GEORGE  N

DANGEROUS WAYS

A MEMOIR

CRANTHORPE
MILLNER
PUBLISHERS

First published by Cranthorpe Millner Publishers (2023)

ISBN 978-1-80378-154-9 (Hardback)

www.cranthorpemillner.com

Cranthorpe Millner Publishers

FOR VIRGINIA

CONTENTS

PART ONE

PART TWO

PART ONE

CHAPTER I

A HOME OF SAND

It was on my sixth birthday, on "the glorious twelfth" of August, that we docked in Africa. It was a moment of transition. Deposited in Malta by a liner on its way to India, we had waited in a makeshift transit camp for any passing vessel that was going on to Libya. Maybe a week or two weeks later we were salvaged by a little cargo ship, whose only passengers we became. Down below, in the queasy roll and swelter of our cabin, sleep eluded us. But my mother's importunity with the captain, a process with the opposite sex in which as time went on she grew adept, provided a solution. For the three nights following we lay back at our ease in hammocks on the open deck, where nothing stood between us and the heavens' brilliance.

The next day we reached Tobruk and all its shattered devastation, steering our way among the wreckage – the broken ships still visible and all their sorry fellows down below. To a child of my age it was a spectacle perhaps emotionally indifferent though certainly arresting.

My father was on the quay to meet us. I have the instant evidence of this transformative encounter. It's an unmounted photograph, in black and white, kept indiscriminately with some others in an envelope. Our photographer may have been a fellow officer or a sergeant, or the blond German prisoner of war assigned to us as a domestic servant for whom in return we served as stand-in family. Behind us is the ship's ladder down which we have just descended to our future; to the side behind us and part chopped out of view appears the trunk containing our possessions and our closed up past in England. On the left of picture stands my father in his khaki uniform, in military shorts and stockings, and a hat whose mass and girth appear to weigh on him. He is, unusually, smiling outwards from – one would have said – inside himself, with an air of being finally complete. He is holding my sister up beside him. Next to him my mother also smiles, but enigmatically sideways. I stand beyond my mother, my arms hanging stiffly from my sides, my feet turned in towards my mother's. My sister's eyes, like mine, are staring out in front of them, not at the camera or the person holding it, but it would seem our own confusion and anxiety. As a dishevelled token of our journey, my mother's and my sister's hair stands roughly off, fluffed up, in all directions from their heads.

Here in Tobruk I was to learn I couldn't just assume, as I always had in England, that I'd be found acceptable.

4

And by my father, it would transpire, I wasn't. On his pair of scales my faults weighed down my merits with judicial emphasis. And yet my few short months in Libya were a time in which my eyes were opened to new visions and new interests.

Soon we had left the harbour and the damaged town behind us on a road or track which may have had some tar on it but would more likely have been hardened sand. Instead of what I had come from, a piece of rural country of low hills and shallow valleys broken up industrially by brick, there were the barren gritty slopes and flats of a desert that had almost reached its end. Gradually climbing, we reached a solitary building by the road. Its outlook contained no others, only the variegated gradients of scrubby desert and a sky of its usual blue. This was to be our house. Low and narrow, it had been built for our arrival. On a peninsula, it had nothing beyond it but eventually the sea. In my own mind, that is, there was nothing, since we never ventured far along the rising slope behind us. Sometimes the Bedouin, with their hens and donkeys, went by up or down it in their visits to the harbour. I don't recall that I was ever greatly curious about that unseen hinterland. It's only since then, at sudden unprepared for moments, I have felt regret I never crossed it to its unknown ending. It would have been to have removed the burden of its mystery, but also the scope for making my ideal image of it.

Our garden was a virgin plot of stony desert sand,

without a plant or bush or tree, which had been demarcated by a low stone wall built round it by the army. There was room, however, for ambition in that desert waste, and the circuit of the wall was generous. Indeed, the ground plan for the enclosure's horticultural fruition was in place. Chiselled pieces of white stone, immaculate though rough-surfaced, had been arranged in straight or curving lines which seemed to point towards the laying down of paths and flower beds. Each set of stones possessed its own dimensions; some larger and some smaller, indicative, undoubtedly, of structural importance. They might have been awaiting substitution by the hedges of a parterre – a *jardin à la française*. You had before your eyes perhaps the embryo of a diminutive Versailles or Villandry. And, since in our time there not a single stalk came through, inchoateness was to prove our garden's destiny.

It was, though, up a little way beyond us on the higher ground, where rock took over from the sand, that tiny flowers emerged through openings even finer. Their faint, elusive scent which seems sometimes almost on the edge of coming back never, however, quite achieves this, and I am left to feel that while I have perhaps its essence its substance lies beyond me. Perhaps I must await some trigger from elsewhere – some other sensation or experience – that can press it back to life?

There was no school for me to go to because apart from me, my sister being only two, there would have been no pupil. For a while, however, perhaps only from September when at home the school term would have started, I was taken in the mornings to the office of a short and round and jolly sergeant, who fitted me among his other jobs in teaching me some English and arithmetic, but whose lasting pedagogical achievement was to show me how to make a paper aeroplane. And in my final visit he gave way to what had always been my longing and let me build my aircraft from a special yellow paper, of which his stock was limited and kept for something way above my purview, namely "key official documents". That to please me he surrendered was an indulgence of the kind that finds its monument among one's private debts.

The military environment had become a part of me, or what I saw all round me. And so it was one afternoon I set off with two soldiers engaged in the disposal out at sea of land mines and related hazards in which the area was littered. The sun as always shone, and I sat on the pontoon boat with them as it steered a course well clear of wreckage I had seen on my arrival. These two were cheerful, friendly men who like me were wearing only shorts, though one had on a beret and the other had grown a beard. Their lean bodies were bronzed and muscled by exposure and exertion. The ease with which they jettisoned their cargo matched that of their disposition, and, the deck now bare, we made a genial return to shore.

All these years later the coast I partly knew is still

7

bestrewn with danger, not only from different later wars involving different parties but from that very time when I was living there in the contamination. On the road out of the town towards the west you passed the metal remnants, stacked chaotically together in their smashed up post-existence, of the tanks and fighter planes that had disputed land and sky. Whether these tarnished corpses were an unhappy marriage of the Allied and the Axis interests I have no recall and perhaps was never told. I have, however, a photograph of a tank of unknown type, less damaged than the majority, on which I am standing with my little sister face on to the camera: I, left, by the open hatch, my sister, right, above me on the turret behind what seems to be a double barrel.

This ordnance mortuary was the first encounter that the road to Derna set in front of us. Beyond the mangled and dismembered carcases the road continued, shimmering, on the sandy flat that, where to our right it met the sea, was fractured by uneven, rough-edged infiltrations. And then it turned away to climb up the escarpment, which it was obliged to manage, via many windings, tortuously until it had come out on the top and was in a corrugated world of ledges from which the sea, so far below, appeared and went, its motion as of a being only half awake...[1] It was so long a journey that when,

---

[1] *Out at sea the dawn wind*
    Wrinkles and slides.
    T.S. Eliot, "East Coker", *Four Quartets*, Faber & Faber

in the distance way beneath us as we were turning inward round a bend, some dazzling buildings, lit by the sun, appeared, it was as if we were nearly there, desire giving weight to my illusion.

Our hotel was in the heart of Derna – a square of European architecture built by the Italians. Old fig trees stood between the buildings and its centre, to part of which they gave protection. And through the fastened shutters of our rooms, which now were filling up with shadow, there broke the sharp impatient horns of cars and taxis. Their acuteness offered an unlikely comfort as it came to join us when the sun was going. Its resonance I soon associated with North Africa, and if I have ever heard it echoed elsewhere, perhaps in European towns or cities, it has been as if it weren't the same sound I was hearing but a spurious copy.

Not much of Derna is required to suggest its complex history, its variety of occupiers, cultures and ascendancies. Modern European settlement, as reflected in our hotel, had been, when we were there, a matter of less than forty years. But adjacent to our square, and just outside it, was the Bedouin *souq* or *souk*, reflective of a more abiding occupation and more genuine possession of the country. This market, shielded from the brilliance outside, you went into as into a tunnel whose absolute darkness was relieved by lamps. Other pre-modern penetration, by the Greeks and Romans, had left its architectural impression all along that sea coast, but concentrated nearer Tripoli.

9

Beyond Derna, when we were coming from Benghazi on another journey and after many hours had reached the early evening, we had paused a few moments at what must have been Cyrene but which I remember always, having been half-asleep, as by the sea, where is only to be found its port, the vanished Apollonia.

We visited also, perhaps with Dr Barber (who has left his mark upon me), those caves in Derna to which the residents, over the course of 1941 and 1942, had fled for shelter from continuous bombardments as power passed between the Axis and the Allied forces. These bare and open caves had left for time's inspection such traces as an iron rusting on its ironing board, as well as other scattered chattels and utensils.

I don't remember whether Dr Barber, though civilian, was my father's colleague in any way, or a friend, or no more than an acquaintance, but an accident one early morning in our bathroom called for his attention to me. I had been alone there with my sister, my parents being still asleep. Having it to ourselves, we had it as a place to reconnoitre. It was a world entirely new to us of marble, porcelain and chrome, whose abstruse functions and procedures bore only an oblique relation to their basic military equivalents at home. Unlike our bathroom in Tobruk, which had one single basin for the face and hands, the hotel's had two, the second being on the floor and clearly, it was my deduction, for the feet. It had, like the other, two taps. Before I stepped up into it I found the water coming from the hot tap was too hot and even scalding, and therefore settled on the other's, which gushed obsequiously about my toes; as I stood there wallowing in this unwonted luxury, all at once, unbearably, I felt a burning pain and fell out backwards to the marble floor. My sister down below, unseen by me above, had acted, I imagine, in a spirit of uncomprehending solidarity. My head had been cracked open, which was, it emerged, a task for Dr Barber. I had become a subject for his own experimental view of treating head wounds in which stitches had no function and some other means of suture was adopted whose nature I was never told or learned, although the spot remains, hidden within my hair, a bald one; and of Dr Barber's ingenuity I became the ineradicable evidence.

How my attendance at his surgery, or it may have been *in situ* treatment of me, was related to our visit to his house and family is another detail long forgotten, though my going there had a number of effects that were more durable than a detail. Their house was a kind of intermediary through which one rambled from the front, which was on an even level, with a swing on which the Barber girls would rise to Fragonardian heights, and the back, which led to a garden of indigenous intensity. It was a property catering not only for the human sort of being but the feline, and there were various having the run of it. It was the beginning of my love of cats, first realised in our cat in Egypt, a tortoise-shell half Siamese and half of unknown provenance. She had been the outcome of an inadvertency.

The house's middle, which was a junction seeming to expand in all directions, had at its heart a dining table. On this the girls had put an album, the first one of its kind I had encountered, and at once, gazing at it as they turned the pages, I was seduced: I had become an instantaneous philatelist. Their stamps were used and of low value, having mostly come off letters sent from Malta, where it appeared they had relations; and so I saw the harbour of Valletta, a citadel, a ship and a cathedral, and the great prize in their collection, the 5/- green from which emerged the three sides of the palace square. Apart from these there were some little British stamps which I had come across in England, but not with the mysterious letters M.E.F. upon them; and they had also one or two Egyptian stamps depicting King Farouk. It was enough to form a passion.

The garden at the back, which fell away quite steeply from the house, was more of a vernacular arboretum whose trees, near neighbours to each other, bore oranges and lemons. I descended through them to a massive wall behind which, way below, the waves of Mare Nostrum crashed and thundered. I had a longing there and then to have possession of this garden in which you had both heat and shade together, while mysteriously and remorselessly, and entirely out of sight, the sea beat up against the stone foundations.

It was the briefest of encounters in which to set in place three lasting passions. In my own garden in

Tobruk there were no cats, but there were a pair of hens, given me, I understood, by the local Bedouin perhaps to compensate me for my isolation. These and a pair of tortoises were my companions with whom I shared my thoughts and feelings. At night the hens retired to a house of cardboard made for them, I imagine, by my German friend whose name was Jupp and blond hair swept back by a comb he brought out regularly from his uniform. It was most commonly after supper, when my forces had been so often scattered by my father's reappearance, that I sought comfort, as the night was falling and the sky was lighting up, squeezed in with them inside its walls.

These brief moments, from a time which in itself was short and is now so distant, come easily and sharply into focus, giving the past, thus concentrated and reduced, a feeling of immediacy that the present may all too often seem to lack.

My father having been posted, we sailed along the coast to Egypt. I took with me my tortoises, but secretly, and kept them in a cabin drawer. Discovered in Port Said, they proved to be in breach of entry regulations and were, without my knowledge, confiscated. I gathered later that they had been released to pass their last years in the transit camp, where once again we waited to address our future.

I signalled earlier my discomforts with my father. How should I account for our joint failure, which for a long time I wished and thought could be got over but

13

finally I accepted as inevitable and unchangeable? Was I guilty of not immediately loving a father of whom I was immediately in fear, a stranger from whom I was immediately estranged? Did I, that very first day, make all appropriate efforts to be reassuring to him, so that he could know beyond all doubting that hereafter, though till now I had loved my mother only (and also her mother and her sister), he would weigh equally with her in my affections and considerations, as on a pair of scales? Was it this lack of reaching out which, intensifying as I was punished for it, only aggravated the dissociation? My father had discerned he had an unlicked rival, one who had seized advantage from his absence, which had in no way been to serve himself but in the service of his country. My intimacy with my mother chilled my father, to which his riposte was not to seek to replicate that intimacy but rather to punish me for my enjoyment of it and my continuing dependence on his wife. Wasn't he by now a man of power and standing in the army and a doctor in a line of doctors of as many generations as I had managed yet of years? Wasn't he long accustomed to the issuing of orders with which compliance must be automatic? But I had come out on parade with gaiters unblancoed and moreover, it appeared, indifferent to the drill. There was nothing about me that suggested military potential. My father, clipped in moustache and manner, would have perceived me disappointedly, undergoing even nausea at my instinctive reference to my mother whenever I felt anxious or, on the other hand, was pleased. He had made of me, in his presence, someone muted – deadened. The spontaneity I felt with those I loved was absent.

CHAPTER II

CAMPING OUT

My father had been posted to the garrison of Fayid (Fayed), at a strategic point on the Canal beside the Bitter Lakes, half way between Port Said and Suez. After perhaps a fortnight in the transit camp, a place of tents pegged into an expanse of grass, we left for our new home and quarter.

Between our lives in Libya and Egypt there was both continuity and disconnection. There were the continuities of the desert and the British military presence, though socially, domestically and educationally we were in another world. And yet, in however different circumstances, at Fayid we were returning in some measure to a previous existence of the kind that we had known in England. We were no longer, as in Libya we had been, generally cut off from women or from other children, and there was the further comfort, which in England had been lacking, that wives were here cohabiting with their husbands rather than being separated from them by the war or post-war aftermath.

Fayid, as it was then spelt and which was to be our home, was a major camp divided into many sectors whose symmetries I never knew because into so much of it I never had reason to enter. Respectful of the natural association of like people, and conversely separation of the unlike, rank in the army was the determinant of individual geography. Yet the building specifications for the officers' or sergeants' or the other ranks' accommodation couldn't have much differed if their apex was the minimalism of the officers' family quarters, whose narrow one-storey brick and timber blocks had in each of them four families or couples lacking kitchens (meals being taken centrally in rank-based dining halls). They were dimensions which in that intensity of heat required temperate behaviour, with everyone pressed up against each other in a way allowing little scope for privacy but making large demands on tolerance. We were, however, privileged. In other camps accommodation might come down to tents, in which you either froze or boiled, a matter to which ultimately Parliament gave its ineffectual attention.

Our own block was on the camp's perimeter and looking out as if towards our freedom. The road ran slightly down beyond us to a view of undeveloped sand, and perhaps there might have been some threadbare saplings planted at the side of it. From here, as I recall,

17

it wasn't long before you reached the Great, or larger, Bitter Lake, a vast expanse of salty water across which in the distance, from the beach or on the jetty, you might catch sight of ships which might be waiting with their anchors down or else be moving forward on their way to India or England or some other far off place, though whether they were waiting or were moving was never quite apparent.

Our neighbours to the left of us, as you looked towards the road, became, in the way sometimes of army people meeting overseas, my parents' friends. Childless, and retiring afterwards to Bournemouth, the Naylors took up cocker spaniels, of which they made their family. Having got to it before us, they were already settled in the end accommodation. This had an extra patch of garden that was inundated daily from a truck that came round with the so-called water wallah. Their sunflowers, pampered by such drenchings, rose imperiously above my head, and at the more modest level of my feet the earth had vanished underneath petunias, of which my favourites, purple-blue in colour, had a velvet texture and were the only ones that, if you leant right down so that you almost touched them, filled you, nearly beyond your breath's capacity to absorb it, with their perfume. Their sweetness even came to meet you as you walked towards them. Not only in their memory but in a spirit of continuation, it is these same petunias that I plant each summer in my English garden, whether in bowls outside my windows on the gravel or in planters even nearer to me on the window-sills.

I was, not yet a gardener, envious of this little extra piece of land of which they made intensive use and which conferred on them an aura of superiority. This was despite my father's being senior. Major Naylor, however, had arrived there first and naturally abhorred a vacuum. Nor did it ever strike me, since I never heard my parents mention it, that my father was entitled to the Naylors' quarter. There is little that is litigious in my cautious instincts. My nature leans towards passivity and 'hoping for the best', such optimism going with a trust that my instinctual inertia will suffice to keep me out of danger. My father, however, was to be revisited, later on in England, by similar ill luck regarding army houses, for there another lieutenant-colonel, nominally answerable to my father, had beaten him to the quarter meant for the Commanding Officer, which had an extra ground floor room, designated by his offspring as the study, into which I was invited by them sometimes as a pointed favour.

Major Naylor, like my father, sported a moustache, but one less clipped than putting out branches at its ends. He was a biggish man with reddish-purple cheeks and eyes disproportionately on the small side which looked out warily as if, should you provoke him, they might turn nasty. I sought therefore to keep always on his right side, except for one occasion, which I shall come to, where I feared his disapproval, though his reaction was quite different from the one I feared.

Our unprepossessing homes had no verandah, only the shade provided by an overhanging roof, beneath which was a concrete base or pavement. This lacked, however, a kerb but was on the level of the earth and sand and grit beyond it. Here, for your comfort, you might set out chairs and have your tea or lemonade – or, if you were Major Naylor or my father, your evening beer or whisky. It was a place for observation, whether your interest was geology or entomology. In the distance, on the left hand of the successive corrugated metal roofs that stretched in front of you and glittered dazzlingly all day, there rose the only feature locally of any height and for that very reason called a 'mountain' although it had the sounder name of 'Flea'. With its greyish colour that was always faint, it had for me a charm that was unfailing as it stood there in its slight and self-effacing way above the general flatness, and perhaps I owe to it the greater partiality I have always felt for hills than mountains.

If, however, I looked downwards I might be greeted with a panorama more sporadic than that afforded by the Flea but, I would find, more gripping. Now I had become a god, observing from above, and as detached from what was going on below me as, paring his fingernails, a novelist such as Joyce might claim to be from characters he had invented. Clearly, I might intervene if I so chose, and change the action or the personnel: I might save some big ants from their small and vicious killers. Instead, I left them to their cruel fate, to be carried off by tiny soldiers to some buried camp and there, presumably, consumed for breakfast, lunch or dinner. Always I had power to be merciful and also power not to interfere with what was foreordained. Invariably I chose to watch the Roman or the Spanish spectacle, dispensing with the importunities of a compassion which is ineffectual.

Able to relish conflict in the role of a spectator, my nature is averse to being part of it. And yet it has a tendency to find itself involved against its will and purpose. Of the four primary schools I attended I had fights in two, although it was in the last, where I was most at home, that I endured, buried within a screaming mob, a creditable draw.

It was at the Army school in Fayid that I had the first of them. The school was in walking distance of our block. Just beyond us, as it was entering the camp, the road curved round towards the left and made a straight line up towards the school. In doing so it passed by all the playing fields, which were on its right. The school itself was visible beyond them. Quadrangular in form, it was some distance from the roadside entrance gates, to which it stood end on. Near to the building was a sand pit of deceptive innocence which was the locus of a squaring up whose cause I have forgotten. Of short duration, it ended graphically in my triumph, from which I backed away in horror. Within moments I was retreating from the school and down the road to a cupboard in my parents' bedroom where, shutting the door against the world, I cowered fearfully. Before my eyes gushed out my victim's blood, and in my ears rose up the furious clamour for my seizure. I was, however, soon evacuated from my cupboard and escorted back to school by Major Naylor, who had chanced to be at home. He walked along with me in silence, projecting no emotion, whether sympathetic or condemnatory, but with judicial impartiality. He may even have been taking, with a discretion proper to the circumstance, bemused pleasure in the outcome, which, whatever might be done about it, might be deemed to prove my mettle. I recall, however, no consequence of any kind.

I was subject, towards the end of our two years in Egypt, to a different kind of battle. This time it was with a teacher. It was a misleading entrée to a love affair, not with the teacher certainly but with the underlying rationale for our encounter, a product of the modern history of Egypt and its diversity of cultural ingredients, in which the French and English had contemporary prominence. However far French teaching had progressed in English primary schools by 1950, it had made its way into the language diet of the British Army child in Egypt. This was without foresight or anticipation of the Anglo-French entente of 1956. More importantly for me, my impasse with the teacher might have jeopardised what proved to be in time, from its obscure beginnings in her classroom, the growth of an infatuation both with French and France.

Whether as a core or optional subject, at the age of

seven I was learning French. The battle's nature has scored into me where I was sitting: in the second row from the right, three places from the front. The door to the outside – which consisted of a verandah and beyond it an interior square of sand – was half way down the classroom's right as one looked towards the blackboard and our fearsome teacher, a French lady of some physical and also mental substance and *d'un certain âge*. Having no insight into what might constitute a typical Frenchwoman, who I would discover later was in certain English eyes petite and elegant and understated, other than in itself it didn't much affect me that this teacher seemed, whether in her imposing superstructure or the hard grinding of her voice, to have been constructed out of granite, from which I might so easily, as I suspect I did, have formed too early and misleading an impression of our Latin neighbours.

Having suddenly a sharp need to be excused I asked for her permission, which she denied me, I would suppose *par habitude*. For a little while I waited in an anxiety whose acuteness rapidly intensified. And then a climactic moment came which ended my deliberation. Jumping up, I fled around the barricade of intervening desks and rushed out through the open door.

Afterwards I went back again, relieved but also apprehensive. My behaviour, however, was left unquestioned. She must have been, though a hard, a realistic and pragmatic woman who understood from long practice the balance of her interests.

23

The incident, which after all had left me with a feeling of achievement, proved only a stumble on the road that took me, as the years went by, ever closer to the Gallic world. Later, at school in England when I took up French again, I came across a painting by a Frenchman in the grammar book, where the girl, in all her frills, is riding high among the foliage and branches. There was, in the moment caught there, a type of light abandon unfamiliar to my English nature. The grey milieu, however, of a textbook, where all is economical, had drained it to its shadow, so that when long afterwards I caught up finally with the original, among its fellow paintings in a London square, I was amazed and even disconcerted by its startling luminosity.

It wasn't, however, a painting that made of me – bar politics – a Francophile. France has, for an Englishman who feels not quite complete in Englishness, a power never weakening. It has its paysage and its literature, its music and its painting, all of which have made their inputs to me. Yet I was captured firstly, soon after my meeting with the Fragonard, not by the country or its arts but by a living woman twice my age, she being, I gathered, twenty-eight whereas I, an adolescent English visitor to her parents' grandiose *domaine*, had only just become fifteen. Odile at once prescribed the standard in my mind for unattainable women, or inserted in me the anxiety that all such women must be unattainable. The devastating composition of her features was made if possible more awesome by a distant manner which could not be melted. She impressed me as superior in form and spirit. Doubtless enhancing these effects, not only was her family rich in a manner I was unused to but she was also married with two children still no more than infants. Her husband was a man already going bald who, one day when I was with them on the bank of their *étang*, proclaimed, with a dreaminess entirely unabashed, his love for her in a song that was like an inward murmur to which I listened as a fellow lover, and with the yearning of one unloved. And also, as an inhibited English boy, I admired his insouciance. It was this second Gallic woman, who like the first showed no regard for me, who brought on my *affaire de coeur* with France. The only thing I ever heard her say about me was to the family's doctor when he was stitching stitches in my head (smashed open untowardly against the floor of their *piscine*). It was a remark that, whether it placed me or misplaced me, lodged for ever in my English consciousness:

'Comme il est flegmatique, comme tous les Anglais.'[2]

It showed how great was the abyss between us, and how I must be of such small note to her and must be reconciled to being. I was, however, comforted to think she seemed oblivious of my true condition. Hereafter I could only want those women I despaired of ever having, a condition which by way of its extremity may

---

[2] 'How phlegmatic he is, like all the English.'

sometimes lead us to possession.

If one is English and loves France presumably one must love the landscape even if not engaging with the language. Nor may French people matter greatly to one's love of France. In my own case both the language and the French people I have met and known have been organic parts of my affair with it. There was, however, no successor to Odile, except perhaps in literature: in Flaubert, Proust and Alain-Fournier, the deep masters of romance. I have always liked the fact of Odile's being as a name so very like Odette, although there was nothing in Odile of the cocotte, at least in what she let me see of her, which was very little.

*

But I have wandered away from Egypt and the Army classroom...

Fayid was on a more or less straight line which goes by road and by canal between the ports of Suez and Port Said. Because of this I think of all our journeys as of going up and down.

On this straight line there was the railway also. Over time, however, the locomotives and their coaches rotted in the very spots where years before they'd been left standing, until there were no longer any rail connections north and south or east and west, so that it wasn't any longer possible to take a train from Ismailia to Cairo or Suez to Port Said or Cairo. But time has redeemed its

26

losses, and these days happily the railways are again in place.

I no longer remember which the trains were going by us as we proceeded on the road or on which canal bank was the railway or, the only time we went by train, which station we were setting off from or returning to from Cairo. It seems most likely it was Ismailia, but may not have been. Nor can I remember the alignments, which at different places will have varied between the road, the railway and the two canals, although I can envisage even now the two canals on either side of us: the Suez to the east and the said Sweet Water to the west. The railway may have crossed from Sinai at a spot called El Qantara, but whether this was in our time or previous to or after it is yet another of those details either lost to me or never known. Nor was I aware in those days that the latter of these canals turned off due west to Cairo when, having come up from the south, it arrived at Ismailia, which may be an instance of new knowledge making up for other losses, though the losses bear along with them perhaps the larger interest of their mystery. There can be more substance in a question than in the things to which we have the answers.

Sinai, on the other side of the canal, was an always present desert, in different lights a reddish- or a yellow-brown and universally a tawny waste with barren rises into hills; perhaps, if El Qantara were behind you as you drove towards Port Said, you might pass by on an embankment an immobile or an almost stationary train.

In all this desert that we lived in there was also, even not far off from our doorstep, a great quantity of water. During afternoons there was the lake to swim in: from the elongated jetty to the little ring for the inexpert or the further raft for the more seasoned. In the distance you might spot the bony tankers, like upturned rakes, or the svelte figures of the liners in the midst of lonely journeys from beginnings quite unknown to endings equally unknowable. Or at Ismailia there was the smaller lake called Timsah, which unlike the other was a shallow adjunct where the ships, as they eased by, might seem to be standing almost over you as their passengers who had come to line the decks, but were further from you than perhaps you thought, called out their greetings, which remained inaudible. And on the road when we were coming near Port Said, or possibly it was Cairo, I recall a sudden view, which filled up all the windscreen, of a blue and glistening piece of water on which the yachts were turning, and at the very fringe the lofty foliage of the palms and other overhanging trees whose brilliant deep green was being caught in evening sunlight. It was a vision of a moment that the road immediately removed, all views to it being equally indifferent.

One of the glories of the beaches at Port Fouad and at Fayid was the lack of buildings other than small huts or shelters stocked with a few refreshments such as beer or lemonade or Coca-Cola. They were structures modest enough to be forgotten. Only at Timsah was there the greater substance, which also was unassuming, of the British Club. My memory of Suez, visited with my parents, is another matter. We were at the strategic junction of the canal with the Red Sea, in an upper room of no great size which, if you looked downwards from the expansive window circling round it (for the room was circular), appeared to be marooned in water. We were in a salon for the meeting of the Occident and Orient, nestling in English armchairs drinking Turkish coffee, which was very rich and sweet, from tiny, delicately painted china cups. Meanwhile my parents chatted amiably with our host, the British Consul, of whom my memory resurrects a tall and lean patrician whose unerring waves of silver hair were marshalled as if on a parade ground, and still, from so far off, makes audible his muted plummy tones crammed full of luscious juices.

As for other cities, of Port Said I recall particularly the contrast, instantaneously effected as the door was opened, between the furnace of the streets from which we were retreating and the interior of Simon Arzt, which met us like an opulent and hushed refrigerator. Our one visit to Cairo was, as earlier noted, the only time I think I went by train. Possibly we had come on it from Ismailia, or it might have been Tel-el-Kebir, a camp out in the desert, or otherwise from Fayid, through which the railway made its way to Suez. In Cairo, naturally, we visited the Pyramids and Sphinx, and also its Museum, whose reverential lighting glinted off the cabinets' glass frontages and black and gold incumbents.

Two other perspectives linger on from Cairo: the first, when, I imagine, we were in the city's very heart, low down among tall buildings which were dark and shadowy in light fading to a glimmer, and I was looking up their faces at the growing night; the other, when we were leaving from the central station while all across it, at other somnolent platforms, darkened carriages stood empty.

One sticks together memories like loose stamps in an album. They are a few bright images which are separated from each other by a seeming void, as if in all our other time we had not, perhaps, existed. Is it only what I manage to remember that continues to exist? Yet some memories, that are not forgotten but suppressed, are those we could most easily recall if only our cruel purpose were to hurt ourselves.

As military families we lived, in almost every sense, apart, inside our own communities. Our contact with Egyptians was to a very large degree transactional, its focus on domestic service and related menial functions. Of their middle and professional classes I saw little, unless – which rarely happened – we were walking in the central portion of a city, whether Ismailia or Port Said. And each experience was like a new event, and they appeared again as unknown quantities, novelties to be gazed at in the flow of their aplomb, in their made-to-measure suits, their fezzes and dark glasses and their glossy limousines. It was each time a reminder that, beyond the desert camps and roads, there was another world to which I had so little access. But on the road accompanying the canal we could observe the mass of poorer people as they passed us on their buses or their lorries or their bicycles or donkeys or on simple foot, all which proximities, as a Christian and a British officer, my father saw as traffic hazards.

I had little if any consciousness of politics or of the nature of the politics containing us in Egypt. In the years I lived in Egypt we were using up the last of our Imperial time. We were living, without much noting it, in the rump of our hegemony; if we saw our sinking case, largely we disregarded it. For in the Egypt beyond our camps post-war radicalism, both military and religious and in concert, was taking hold. The light of trust, such as it was, was going out. All this was far beyond my grasp.

My father returned to Egypt for a second tour of duty early on in 1954, after a year or so in the Sudan. By now tensions had been accumulating. While he had been in London there had been a *coup d'état* which had displaced the monarchy. Egypt was now a military republic. The standing Treaty that had provided for a British presence up to 1956 had been annulled. As British forces stayed, however, guerrilla actions hardened. Britain was obliged to reinforce its garrisons with national service conscripts, boys who having only just left school were picked off more or less as they arrived. The canal road had become a place of carnage. This was the same road that for years had seemed a place the British fronted, as if on centre stage, while its indigenous inhabitants provided an amorphous backcloth. But anonymity became now advantageous. The will to send the British packing was in the hands of those who were invisible.

From school in London I went twice more to Egypt, in 1954 and 1955, the first time to an army camp half-way across the desert separating Ismailia from Cairo. Tel-el-Kebir was where I spent my summer holidays. I don't suppose I knew that this was where in 1882, defending a canal not long since opened but already recognised as vital to its interests, Great Britain had defeated the Egyptian forces and restored the Khedive.

The second time was to a garrison adjoining Ismailia, a city it had become too dangerous to enter. I was to find that journeys on the road with which I once had been familiar and had found less stressful than fatiguing, were now accompanied by rifles and a soldier escort, who would be sitting in the front, and that, though he never let me see it, my father had his own revolver with him in a khaki holster.

Prior to both these visits my anxieties had been resting not on the dangers lower down but on where I sat alert now in the utter darkness of a cabin all of whose lights had been extinguished, a passenger in a piston-engined aircraft – a York perhaps or a Dakota – while, low in the dark night sky, it continued in its onward wandering with disconcerting lurches or sudden abrupt descents, or enigmatic changes in its droning, over a surface that I couldn't see but stared at with the knowledge we were nearly there, until finally – coming up out of nowhere – a light, and then another distant from it, shone but so faintly that they showed me nothing other than themselves as meanwhile the plane insisted on its wavering, until at last it turned, and then it banked determinedly, and turned again, and I saw a moment later in the blackness a pattern of small lights set well apart, but nearer now, which surely marked the boundaries approaching. And then we were coming down, and as the runway lights came up too speedily there was a bump, and then, as the lights now next to me went flashing by, my mind was only on deceleration, which came with a tardy jarring urgency. But the plane stopped, and turned aside, and then set off along the tarmac, clattering in a careful manner, towards low buildings dimly lit. I had arrived again in Egypt, but perhaps not truly conscious of its dangers or its animosity.

*

Only a few years earlier, when I was living there, my father had had amicable dealings with the Egyptian manager of our canteen, and thanks to the rapport between them there had come an afternoon when Osman took me and my little sister with him in his car.

It was a trip to see his village and his family and neighbours, and a little of their way of life. Much like the sunflowers in the Naylors' garden, the vibrant stalks rose far above our heads in great profusion and good health, enjoying all the benefits of nourishment from the canal, despite its infamous pollution. I see myself, even as I write this, beneath a pure blue sky, standing at the side of Osman, while on his other side he has my sister's little hand in his. He is chatting to his audience, informing them that it is really true we are the colonel's and that we are his little English friends.

I have a photograph of Osman, not in his village but outside a quarter, in a combination of dark trousers and white coat – a tall and well built man with a moustache more generous and cheerful than my father's, and responding to the camera with the authentic smile which never seemed to fail him. He is holding up my sister, with her hair in pretty bunches, as she is standing with much need of him on the diagonal capstone of a concrete post; and I am next to her, but on the opposite diagonal, held upright by a smiling waiter in a sash and fez.

We see the world from the perspective we have, at any moment, come to. To alter it may be a feat of ingenuity, a leap demanded of our understanding for which we may have need of tender help. It may require another's "taking us in hand" and perhaps, for best results, quite literally in hand – if, that is, we are ready to have our hand so taken.

CHAPTER III

"IT WAS NO DREAM: I LAY BROAD WAKING"[3]

We had left the sun of Egypt far behind and were off –
but, in that gloom and rain through which the wonder of
a coast appearing faded with its indistinctness, it felt a
long way off – Gibraltar. Far out we would turn the
corner into a world the Romans knew was near the end
of everything, and having climbed past Portugal and
Spain would strike the Bay of Biscay: a brisk welcome
to a new life for which I lacked the programme notes.
For nearly two years and a half my dress had been, but
for the mornings when I was at school, a pair of shorts.
Exposure to those neighbours, the suns of Libya and
Egypt, had painted over my off-white base and left me,
for a moment, a deep, assimilated shade of brown,
which as it also turned my blond hair blonder might
have misled me into thinking this was how I was to be.
And all my life since has had in it the frustrated object

---

[3] Sir Thomas Wyatt (1503-1542)

of that colour's reinstatement.

In this condition as an eight-year-old I found myself again in northern England. It was not our proper destination but a stopping place, and yet a place in which, though it has taken me till now – so far away from then – to see this, my adult life began. We were on our way more permanently to an unknown quantity called southern England and in particular that bit of it made up of northern Surrey and south London which is neither Surrey proper nor is London. My father was returning, but by no means finally, from the command of hospitals, which seemed to offer him a penitential kind of satisfaction, and was revisiting his previous stamping ground, a place mysterious and important, about whose details he was unforthcoming. The War Office, I learned, however, from my mother, had recalled him to its bosom. He became now a commuter from the city's outer edges and chose a town which had three stations going to it. Here he found a rented house to live in while he looked for one to buy. Both, which were far apart, were a short walk along a pavement from their stations. His mind was practical and functional, little deflected by aesthetics, as foreign a world to him as physics has been to me. Both these houses, modern or nearly modern, replicated perfectly on either side and opposite, gazed out on treeless roads called avenues.

First, however, as I gleaned much later, probably also from my mother, my father had a northern mission: to be reconciled, if such a thing were possible, with his father after so many years' estrangement. He must have got in touch from Egypt armed with all those diplomatic ploys that long consideration sometimes gives a letter, although such letters, by being unable to conceal their latent grudges, may prove less curative than fatal. Yet in this instance he succeeded, arriving at the home he had been born in with an escort that consisted of his wife and family. What was his state of mind and purpose? What was it he was expecting other than the opening of old wounds? Did he have some thought of what he might have hoped for from his outstretched hand, given his father's age and aggravated problems with his heart and arteries? Perhaps his mother's death while we had been away had cooled his anger? Were his objectives both emotional and strategic?

My grandfather was now married to the woman who had been his mistress. During this short visit spanning 1949 and 1950 she may have been present as the house's now established mistress or may have been politicly absent, perhaps in that other house she knew much better. Even though as I'm writing, suddenly I see myself, a boy of eight, wandering through the downstairs rooms and corridors and going down some chill stone steps into a kitchen like a hangar whose light was dim and shadowy, to find her there presiding and glancing round sharply as if at an intruder. I have no memory of our speaking to each other, only that I walked by her at a distance, emerging from an outer door into a garage. My descent of those cold stairs had been a Stygian passage to the underworld.

What is, however, certain is that on the first morning of 1950, which was a Sunday, my father's father died. It was a Scottish reel, apparently, which killed him. There was in that a kind of homecoming. His first world had recalled him.

What is also clear to me, now I am far enough away from it to see it, is that a little before that moment or a little after it my eyes were opened, in a manner that was fortuitous and improbable, to my sexuality. I had been separated from my parents and my sister and my little brother and taken down the road a little way and then across it to a very different sort of property, in which my mother's cousin Winifred, known always to me as Auntie Win, lived with her husband Frederick, or Uncle Fred, and their adopted daughter Pauline, who now had reached the age of seventeen, when some girls are becoming women or may feel themselves already women physically and psychologically. There could have been no one who would more readily have had me stay with her than Aunty Win, and Pauline, who had always been so fond of me, was also greatly looking forward to my visit. This my mother must have pointed out as an inducement and a consolation for my temporary exile.

For what particular reason was I separated from my family? Was it because, its being New Year's Eve, my parents and my grandfather were going to a party of the sort one needed to be seen at as a member of the professions or the upper bourgeoisie, and so it was quite properly, they might conceive, a night to give my aunt her own *petite reunion*, when once again I'd stay with her just as, my mother said, I'd loved to do when I was little?

Or was it the next day, which was so unexpected for my parents, finding themselves brought up against the widow in the consequences of this sudden death? I was old enough for my father not to wish me present in such circumstances – not to be concerned with what was not my childish business or within my comprehension, for he seemed always to want to keep me well at bay and in the infantile condition which provoked him, whereas on the other hand my siblings were too young for separation from their mother.

Thus whether the basis was a death or party I was deposited with Auntie Win, who my mother knew from long ago would rush to smother me in her encompassing warm-heartedness. At once I would have sensed the change in atmosphere. I had descended not merely physically from a higher level on that hill but socially. I was breathing in a softer air which came, it must have been, from human sources. It was a little unassuming world of kindness and compassion, of generosity of spirit, which like others before me, not only in life but literature (Philip Pirrip comes to mind), I felt a need, while being drawn to it, to keep my distance from and therefore pushed away – an action which, even as I succumbed to it, I disavowed.

We went in from a yard beside the road, to which the building stood sideways. Facing towards the village down below, it could have benefited from the southern light. You stepped into a room distinct from any I was used to. Wide and bare, its walls a leaden whitish-grey, it had the cavernous feeling of an empty depot. In it, apparently, their lives were mostly led. The low ceiling and the hard unforgiving floor, as well as drab lace curtains screening off the sky, made up a secret world of shadows. On the far side, in the south-east corner, a door opened on a space so limited and dark it might have been a cupboard rather than the room it posed as. Opposite the door there was a narrow bed to which the only access was between it and the door, since on its far side it was up against the wall. There was, though this did not much strike me, a small bedside table with a dim red lamp on it. These were my quarters for the night after an evening, spent largely at the table, full of unaccustomed warmth that eased the stiffness out of me; for I was that evening their compulsive interest. They had so many memories of our times together I had quite forgotten, such as our trips to Scarborough and to Morecambe; and they in turn supplied an audience for my life in Libya and Egypt, at which they either gasped or murmured with amazement. How marvellous Pauleen thought it to have lived in places such as that, with all that glittering sand and sea, which must be why I was so brown and not the pure white little lamb that she remembered. I was grateful to her, though I didn't say so, for this acknowledgement of my improvement, but at the same time wished her memory of me had been less reductive.

As the climax of my tea, which had gone over into supper, my aunt produced a chocolate cake, remembering, she said, my liking for it, which was as I had hoped she would, thinking I might taste again what I had tasted with such pleasure once before. She watched, eagerly and perhaps a little anxiously, my approach to it, and I rewarded her with every semblance of enjoyment. I didn't say, however, in order not to hurt her feelings or appear ungrateful, that this particular chocolate cake entirely lacked the other's flavour and that I had seen at once it would, since the cream that filled it was of actual chocolate, whereas the first's had been a thin white substance the secret of whose uniqueness, although now almost lost to me, seemed still as if it might be found. Perhaps its unassuming essence was that it had been synthetic, the product of a world of rationing.

Now Uncle Fred was standing up preparatory to his withdrawal, but first he asked me if I'd like to help him the next morning with his milk round, though he advised me I would have to stand behind the cab among the crates and bottles, the cab itself being filled up by himself and his assistant. This was a prospect which, while I found it flattering, troubled me in its details. I noticed, which only added to my discomfort, that while explaining this he seemed, from the darting little looks

41

he cast at Auntie Win and Pauline, to find amusement in my quandary.

It was much later now than when I usually went to bed. My aunt said she was afraid my mother would be cross about it if she knew, but there had been so much to talk about, and for both her and Pauline, and Fred as well, she knew, the evening had simply flown. As it seemed my aunt and Pauline meant to go on talking, since Pauline lingered at the table as if awaiting only my departure to continue, I asked my aunt if I could have the door left open so that I could listen just a little longer while I was going off to sleep. This amused her and I think it even touched her, and as a concession to my sociability she left it not quite closed; and I heard them say – quite loud enough for me to overhear it – what a most polite young man I was becoming and how my father must be proud of me, which instead of pleasing saddened me because I greatly feared he wasn't. In time sleep took its hold, and so I missed whatever else they might have said to the advantage of my amour-propre.

*

I found myself awake. My head was no longer where I was certain I had left it, on the pillow, but lying against a countryside on which a pale moon shone. Above, the hills like globes rose swelling round their peaks. Below, a wooded chasm opened, dangerous, mysterious and frightening. I was on the east side of her midlands, south of her heart above me. I was between the wall and Pauline.

I was afraid to move or even breathe, to do anything that would disturb her, thinking she was asleep but afraid also to have found myself beside her undraped body. And in that light, which came from two directions, not only from the moon that shone down through the window but from the table lamp, which for some reason, perhaps for our security, she had left to offer its faint glow, I studied her with fear and pleasure, feeling upon my cheek, now hot, the uncertain refuge of her being. I was alone with my ambiguous sensations, the victim of their duality, which could never be revealed. I was imprisoned in a knot that tied the waking present to the wakened past.

So much of life takes place without an explanation or without our being able later to recall one. We are bound to make of it what we will, which may be wrong or foolish or even right. I was, I had to think, in Pauline's bed and Pauline's room, for reasons perfectly unknown to me. Whether my mother knew of it or how she might have viewed it were not questions I ever raised with her, having learned by now the value of discretion. Besides, in pursuance of their separate motives, it might have been that neither my mother nor my aunt had bothered too much over details. Degrees of candour may require lowering to facilitate agreement. Pauline herself perhaps was a facilitator, having been always so attached to me. And so, until the morning light came up into the window, and then with blunter definition, I was able in effect, though timidly, to study her. As noted, the bed was narrow. Perhaps it was the very one that she had had from childhood. She would have been aware how little room it had in it and must have moved me when she came to bed so that I wasn't lying with her on her pillow but for her greater ease between those parts of her that were for me, however, more intimidating.

Later I was conscious of her getting up and going. I received it as an abandonment. My loss, however, calmed me. Aloneness had restored a feeling of normality.

Soon Auntie Win appeared. She said that I'd been sleeping "like a baby". Uncle Fred had gone down to the dairy but would come back to collect me. Sitting down for breakfast, I couldn't stop myself from looking round for Pauline almost as if I had some right to her and expected her to join me. Did this unease in me convey itself to Auntie Win? For she said that Pauline had had to go to Sheffield and wouldn't be back till later on that evening, long after I had gone, and so had sent me her goodbyes. I had been, in Pauline's words, "just like a statue" in the bed, or "like a cherub... like... a little angel". I was relieved to gather I had not disturbed her, though her comparisons were inglorious. I was more than a cherub or an angel, and was more now to myself than I had been before I shared her bed with her.

Though it was not a matter I had ever heard of, I see

in a closer focus, looking back at this (which I am almost in danger of suspecting never happened, because it seems to me, if suddenly it returns to mind, implausible, and yet I know it did happen, not only because of the transparency with which all these years later I can still recall it but because of its humiliating sequel), the link there was with one of the more notable subjects of Renaissance painting, addressed by painters, Latin and Germanic, in all the studios of Europe: that of a naked Venus with a naked Cupid, a male child of uncertain age and size, whether a vulnerable crying baby in a Cranach, or a complicit smiling boy in a Bronzino. Of these I had been neither – neither quite innocent nor quite guilty.

The early morning, as we rattled over cobbles, was a bracing one. Unused as yet to the cold, I wished I had had thicker clothes like Uncle Fred's assistant. I was, however, better placed in one respect than Uncle Fred had caused me to expect (for he had a Yorkshire sense of humour): as we made our way from street to street, I sat between them in the driver's cab. Each time we stopped I was allowed to carry bottles to the doorsteps, whose whitened surfaces, having been trampled to a bleary residue the day before, seemed all the grubbier for their whitening. It would be only after many years that these cobbled streets we went along in fits and starts would open up their secret to me. It was somewhere in this district that Uncle John had set in train what would become a lifetime's nemesis.

At some point later I rejoined my family up the hill.

45

I have no longer any memory of my mother's questions or my answers. Perhaps I might have talked about the chocolate cake or my adventure on the milk cart, or because I felt a need to mention her, to imply a kind of ownership while heading off all clues to my emotions, I might have added, in a manner that detached her from me altogether, that of Pauline I'd seen little, the sun being barely risen when she'd left for Sheffield.

CHAPTER IV

A HOME FROM HOME

Our life in Surrey lasted for three years until, with painful suddenness, it ended. Surrey is in a way the story of two houses and two schools, but not in the easy tandem this suggests; for while at the first house, which we rented and where our stay was so much shorter, I was a pupil at two different schools, on our removal to the second, which was the one my father bought, the school I went to stayed the same, except that it required another change of journey, the first having been by bus, the next on foot, and the last one making use of both.

This rented house, identical in all essentials to its neighbours on each side, looked slightly down across the road on others wholly similar. My father's walk each weekday morning consisted of two lefts, the first out of the gate, the second, following a little downward slope, at the junction with a bottom avenue whose character was again much like our own. From here my father's unrelenting stride conveyed him to the station.

If, however, your second turn was to the right, a modest distance brought you to a busy road, where if you went left you might eventually reach London, and if the other way, which took you to the High Street, you could emerge at Banstead or, by forking off, at Epsom. On turning left you would at once observe a row of modern red brick shops which were a little way along the other side and had in them a grocer's, where I would take the brown or khaki ration book (from which the grocer's scissors would cut out the "points") on shopping errands for my mother. Next to these shops was a bus stop whence I would begin my life of solitary journeys. Keeping, however, on the near side, you would reach a local council park or recreation ground in which, a short way from its gate, were tennis courts, a bowling green and a pavilion, and beyond them pitches and a long expanse of grass or open field which stretched off gradually uphill. It was a place I merely chanced upon. At the beginning, which was early on in January, there might be people playing football, but later, all in white, the tennis players came, replacing winter's reds and blues and greens and muddy brown. I didn't know or ever speak to anyone, and merely wandered here and there as an observer, in a state of half-expectancy or semi-boredom, or, if I noticed someone coming up to me, anxiety about my lack of standing.

The distance I have travelled now from both of them leads me at times to muddle up this park in Surrey with another, earlier one in Yorkshire I had gone to with my mother. It must be because the ways to these two parks as well as their appearances were similar enough for them to merge into each other in my memory.

If, turning left out of our avenue in Yorkshire, you went into the road beyond, and then continued past the traffic lights, and then proceeded on again past all the warehouses and factories, you reached finally, on your left, a park in which not far beyond the gate were tennis courts, a bowling green and a pavilion, as well as lawns much like the ones in Surrey. Here there was additionally a boating lake, and also, at the back, a little railway bridge that stood within a frame of trees. A path went underneath this bridge and rose a little towards a glade which had a strange and intimate remoteness, but being so shut off and pressed upon by foliage seemed to conceal some secret threat, as if its air of calm were treacherous, so that the regret I always felt on leaving it was matched by my relief.

This bridge had for a long time almost lost a purpose. Only little goods trains now passed over it, but sparingly, and only for a few more years until the line closed altogether and its rails were lifted. Its journey had always been a short one, back and forth between the neighbouring town – a real town and important one – and ours, whose status was unclear, and had ended in some sidings just behind the mill which, from its grimy windows, scrutinised the traffic underneath. Gradually the railway line acquired a new role as a path among the houses that had been growing up around it, and even now continues, with this altered purpose, on its small embankment overlooking them.   By contrast, the railway line in Surrey has retained its natal function, passing just behind the park and all the way along the border of the town until it curves back to the central station, where as it goes across the points the main line takes it over.   Unlike the open air remains in Yorkshire, this Surrey branch line hides within a cutting, with the effect that, at either of the stations which my father used, there was, in the half-light of the early morning, a steep descent to be negotiated to the platform, and then a climb no less demanding in the evening shadows up again.   This railway's subterranean burrowing has spared it over all its years a sight of the amorphous rash above by which the past has been obliterated.

It was necessary for me to go to school, a matter undertaken by my father privily.   He had, as would be later clear to me, explored the ground and, I gathered from my mother, found himself impressed enough by Mr Wakefield to assign me to his care.   Besides, Mr Wakefield would have told my father, the school he was presiding over was not in fact the one that, by the summer or the autumn, he would be in charge of, but another, now in the course of being built in line with all the best of modern practice, though the foundation, dating back to the Victorians, was actually (he would have reassured him) Church of England.   A break in continuity had followed its unholy demolition from above in 1944, but with the new development would very soon be mended. Thus my attendance at his present school would be in fact a short affair and not a matter greatly to concern my father.

Perhaps, for his part, my father urged him to make more of me than was so far showing on the (he would acknowledge) disappointing surface. And perhaps, as well as his authoritative manner, which would have reassured my father, his name, Wakefield, served as further evidence of dependability. Whether as a part-Yorkshireman he responded to it consciously or quite unconsciously, there was nothing in it not to offer him the confidence he needed. As for me, I was unluckily too young to spot, when it might have given me some comfort, the irony of his bearing such a surname.

The authoritative manner natural to my father would in its turn have caused the other to be certain of his seriousness, though without entirely following its direction. In assuming this commission Mr Wakefield would be taking charge of someone quite unknown to him and guided largely by his own impressions in determining the ways in which I most required "bringing on".

My first day came at my new school, a little later than the term's beginning, so that once again I was a person to be remarked on and inspected. It was the third time I had started during a school year and had yet to coincide with a beginning; and later, when I went away to board, which was the bleakest of my initiations, it was on a cold hard day in January. On this first day I was obliged to walk down to the bus stop and to board the bus on which I would proceed between a half-mile and a mile, but nearer to the latter, and a total of two stops. The first of them, unknown to me, was to turn into my stop for going home, whereas my present starting point would find itself without a function, although until that time it weighed on me, each morning as I approached it, as any heavy burden will.

The second stop was at the entry to the High Street, where having left the bus you crossed into a narrow winding lane whose low, mean buildings seemed to press upon you, the slits in them which served as windows balefully opaque. Immediately behind, the town's gasometer, its rusting metal a blotched and streaky yellow-brown, presided. The street's name, Crown, perhaps suggested height and glory, although it was as if it had sunk and closed in from the world beyond. It was a place whose menacing demeanour, from the first moment I was in it, filled me with anxiety.

Was I as a new boy interviewed by Mr Wakefield? I don't recall but think I must have been, since it was on my first or second day's attendance that, at the morning assembly, he introduced me to the school, but in a manner so entirely chilling that my only wish was not to be there – or that I were not myself – or that as I stood there with the others I was unidentifiable – or that his homily were addressed to someone else. I was, though, obliged to listen as he told the school he needed it to help him to amend me. He wished it to address my accent, which, he indicated frankly to his teachers and my fellow pupils, had the ugly flatness of the north of England. This was an introductory humiliation. Others may have followed at the hands of teachers or of pupils, though I have no memory of them, and perhaps there were none, for which I would have felt a hidden gratitude, tempered, however, by my shame at having been so publicly exposed.

Wishing only to suppress the matter of my being found defective, I said nothing about my need of alteration to my parents. If, however, I had done so perhaps at least my mother might have pointed out that Wakefield was the capital of the West Riding. There could have been also other consolations I was too young to know about. I wasn't yet, aged eight, a devotee of Flaubert and therefore could know nothing of Charles Bovary, who on his own first day at school, belatedly at fifteen, had been ridiculed by the master and the class not only for his appearance but behaviour, and as a punishment for such gaucheries had had to copy out *vingt fois,* until they were inscribed upon him as stigmata, *ridiculus sum.* Eventually he had qualified as a doctor and thereby was most unlike me, since my failure to succeed my father in that calling ended what so many Scottish generations had established. As well as not yet knowing of the French boy's shame, so like my own, I was no more familiar, as it might have helped me to be, with the sociology of northern Surrey or the mongrelisation of its rustic accent by a tide of Estuary English.

There was a further discomfort to be lived with in that school, which is the only other memory of it that has stayed with me, the classrooms and the lessons and their teachers having all long faded. This second memory is of break times, when you had to go outside into a yard whose grey-white concrete walls enclosed a rectangle of asphalt, the unruly territory of a group of boys whose shabby clothes and hardened eyes were their insignia of governance. Immediately behind, surveying their brute rule, was the gasometer. Perhaps it was here I first encountered Mulligan.

Early in the summer term the new school opened, receiving pupils from across the neighbourhood. For me the change was an immediate alleviation. The humane new buildings, low to the ground as if to fit in with our own unformed dimensions, had round them open sky and rolling lawns. It was, after a dark age, a renaissance. We were admitted with the kitchen not yet ready, and so instead, as the days grew warmer, sandwiches would be brought in for our lunch, the desks replacing dining tables. It was one of the more agreeable anomalies of all my school experience. This was in the third year class of Mrs Bright, a woman both ethereal and organised with whom my time, passed in the inchoate spirit of a Rossetti or Burne-Jones, was all too soon truncated by the summer holidays.

My new school was much nearer to our house and

not far along the pavement from the bus stop which had intervened between the stops that I'd been getting on and off at. Later it would become the stop for going home. But for the moment there wasn't any need to use the bus. The school was near enough to walk to. Now, on reaching the main road, instead of turning left and crossing over to the bus stop, I went the other way. Here there was a strange configuration such as I had never come across before and never have again. The road proceeded in a cutting that grew ever deeper as it reached its middle and thereafter shallower as it neared the other side. Meanwhile the pavement, which I had been able to remain on, went up steadily beside a smaller road that served a row of houses standing back inside their gardens, until it had reached the level of its peak. Here, at the cutting's greatest depth, there was a bridge of fretted iron where you could walk straight over to the other side as traffic hurtled past you, and as if it were slicing through you if you dared to glance beneath. Sometimes I did, to test myself and to enjoy, the tension over, the pleasure and relief of knowing I was still intact, in one whole piece, an outcome I was for the most part certain of beforehand.

Possibly, on that narrow bridge, your objective was the church, raised on a summit of its own. Here, as the Latin mass proceeded and the censers swung their beatific incense, filling the eyes and noses of the faithful with their burning vapour, there might be interposed a hymn, which might well be, as it rang out: "For all the saints who from their labours rest", since just here it was in effect eponymous, and for the reason that this church and hymn had been united in their dedications as also in the year of their inauguration. What was most remarkable of all, however, about this very glorious hymn was that it had been written by the very cleric whose supreme achievement, at the very end of his career, had been to be appointed to the bishopric of Wakefield, moreover as its first incumbent.

I would, however, disregard the bridge and keep straight on and down the path beyond it to a point where it emerged again beside the London road. And now opposite was the school. I had walked, to reach it, to the top and down the other side of Angel Hill, whose name might also be eponymous in view of the ability it had to raise my spirits, for on my way to school I might encounter other children whom I didn't know or recognise and who showed towards me the complaisance of the angels or of little putti. The claims of a more earthly sort of Angel at the bottom with a link much more historical stood out of sight above my head.

The new school buildings occupied the ending of the slope that ran down from the hill and so were not quite on the flat. As seemed appropriate, the senior forms were at the upper level, looking down across a falling square of grass towards the juniors. The school, all of one storey, was shaped like the letter H, the middle section being given to the washroom and its first headmaster, who was, as he had intimated to my father,

Mr Wakefield. Beyond this central section, at the upper level, was the dining and assembly hall, and lower down were placed the infant classes, an area remote and unrelated. At the inner end of our side was the staff room, which through a window at the back maintained its buried watch upon the playground just above, a precaution built in by the architect which would later prove my saviour.

Our teacher was Mr Stanghan, a man of many unemphatic virtues and one of the earliest of my mentors. He seemed to me middle-aged, which may have been because of his moustache and the withdrawal, just beginning, of his pale brown sandy hair, which he kept immaculately, like his class, in order. Perhaps if I'd been older than I was I might have found him younger, no more than only starting on his middle years. I don't recall he ever raised his voice or had a need to. In his classroom there was a kind of active somnolence. In the first year, when I was sitting somewhere near the middle, I discovered History in Art and Art in History. With our rulers we would divide the pages of our books in four, and then, with all the colours of our sharpened pencils, fill up, it might have been, the first square with Sir Francis Drake, who would be rolling down a bowl, and in the second place Sir Walter Raleigh, who would be laying down his cloak, and in another Queen Elizabeth the First, her face an unearthly chalky white and eyes an unimaginable blue and hair a lustrous halo of pure gold, as if she were no mere mortal but a Church of England saint in heaven.

In my second, which was my last, year in that room I had a desk half hidden in the right-hand corner, from which my eyes could wander through a large patch of the sky. Here on Friday afternoons my mind would drift into a kind of torpor, for it was then he read to us and I would listen, but remotely, to his drowsy voice, which, like radio waves malfunctioning, would fade away and then return again.

One afternoon, awake, I heard the lines

I come from haunts of coot and hern,
I make a sudden sally,
And sparkle out among the fern,
To bicker down a valley...[4]

and understood that whereas "men may come and men may go" that little stream would, in the same meandering manner that it always had, and in a rhythm brooking no dissent, "go on forever".

By now my father had bought the sort of house that he was looking for, one which would do for our accommodation and was very near a station. This was the stop between our previous station and the town's main station, which was still too far away to be of use to him, though later it proved its usefulness to me. Architecturally, we had moved back, I am guessing, from the 1940s to the 1920s. The street we moved to felt more worn, its houses wearier and more cramped

---

[4] Alfred, Lord Tennyson: *The Brook*

and pressed up tight against each other. It was here I was to spend the main part of my life in Surrey.

My father's journeys each morning and evening in and out of London took him from near the exit of our tired avenue to its other further end, which was just before you reached the railway line below, and there he would turn into a narrow alley, fenced in on either side to points above my head, which would bring him to the steps already mentioned. My own walks in the morning and the afternoon, which took me to and from the bus, were rather longer than my father's, nearer to half a mile; as school, however, had turned into a place I felt much more at ease in, my walks through the suburban roads that led into the High Street were taken up with memories or wishes that were largely of the kind that carries you along the pavements less mechanically than mentally.

Each morning I passed by a shop it was my habit to go into coming home on Tuesday afternoons, though sometimes I had already been into the one just near the school. This latter one was opposite a little green, enclosed on three sides by old houses set well back among the trees, and more immediately by a road that circled round it and was where the buses parked and waited. Newsagents such as these were my original suppliers of essentials – in no particular order sweets, which later melted into chocolate, comics, which put on weight as books, and lemonade, decarbonated into claret.

During my first year in the class I had acquired an influential friend who was a year ahead of me and at the year's end would be leaving. He had come to be my friend by means I don't recall, but acted morally as a protector and, as I have come to realise, a guide. He was someone to whom I naturally deferred, though without his ever seeming to expect this. He must, however, have been aware that deference was what I showed him. Not only was he older, he was much bigger, in height and girth, and was the captain of the football team directed by him from the half-back line with much robust solidity. I see him as having been a little bit round-shouldered. His fairish hair came forward on his head and, whether it was trained to do this or was following its inclinations, stuck up at the front in spikes. His chin jutted from his jaw in a manner that was uncommon but familiar to me from my Tuesday reading, where also it was indicative of abnormal muscularity. Like Mr Stanghan he was someone who seemed never to have to raise his voice.

One memory I have of him shows him in his family surroundings. He asked me one day for tea, which proved, like the church above the school, a high one. I was touched and grateful to have been so singled out, as well as curious, perhaps, about his home life. He took me, going behind the green, along a road I vaguely knew that led eventually via others to my own home. Some way along this road we turned and came into a settlement of prefabs, structures quite outside my world.

I had never met and couldn't imagine meeting anyone who lived in them. And yet our school itself was an example of prefabrication, though built perhaps to prove more durable – an aim, however, never tested, its life being prematurely ended this time by its civil demolition. And so the school in which finally I had felt at home would itself prove brittle, replaced beyond my own day by a new one built more solidly and placed at last beside the church whose name it bore.

We had arrived at Alan's house. I followed him inside, into a room much longer than it was broad and almost wholly filled up by a narrow table. Sitting already on both sides and at the ends were clustered, packed convivially against each other in a jumble, the old and young and middle-aged, who at once broke off as I appeared, drawing me in with smiles and murmurs of encouragement. This wasn't my only childhood meeting with the ghost of Dickens. My place, I was glad to see, was next to Alan's, and I was also pleased to be regarded not as a stranger to be questioned but as a guest to be immediately set at ease. It was a room whose psyche seemed oblivious of boundaries or circumstances or distinctions, much as Alan's surname, Bulley, paid no regard to what he was and showed only, if it needed showing, how ill informed is chance.

The visit was a further notice to me of the simple unaffected warmth some people and some families have – perhaps such people as are not constrained by insecurities or by feelings of superiority or a natural coldness. To such approaches, though, I was unable, as I should have wanted, to respond entirely in kind, feelings always the necessity, which had become ingrained in me, of staying on my guard.

Now, in my final year, Alan having left us, another felt able to reveal his colours. Mulligan, whom my friend's name would have better fitted, would most likely have been afraid of Alan, not only physically but of his authority. I myself had gained some standing, being more senior than before and one of those who, in the midday break, was charged with keeping order in the playground. Mulligan, however, as was his need, was spoiling for a fight and looking round for an opponent, a vacancy from which I shied away but to which I found myself incontrovertibly appointed. Mulligan, hard-bodied, had already rounded muscles. He had, additionally, a grey-white skin possessed of a deceptive air of being dead, and eyes that never met your own but looked straight through them as at a vacuity. Against him I was unarguably impotent.

All gathered round us on the unfriendly asphalt. The odds being tellingly in his favour, I was the universal favourite, cheered on by all the boys and even girls, which despite the looming outcome gratified my ego as, manfully but one-sidedly, I struggled where I'd been dragged to, on the ground, finding myself much battered and most copiously knocked about. I don't suppose I landed any blow of note on Mulligan. And yet I held on for "a plucky draw" determined by the advent of two teachers, one of whom marched Mulligan to the Headmaster, no longer Mr Wakefield, who had already left us but with whom my dealings would continue, whereas the other led me in a gratifying spirit of commiseration to the washroom, asking me only how I felt and whether I was hurt at all, in view of which agreeable solicitude I told him that I wasn't. This was a trial from which, unlike its predecessor, where I had had a troubling sort of victory, I could derive some kudos.

One of those who might have watched my struggle was a girl called Christine. She and I and another boy had leading roles in a play the school put on to which our parents came and of which I have a photograph. It shows me sitting with her at a table, and two further girls on either side of us. Standing to the right beyond the table is the other boy. We have the requisite blank faces as we stare out for posterity in the frozen manner of this type of record. My own distinguishing features are an unlit pipe, which I am holding in my mouth, and a dressing gown which at a pinch might represent the garb of a detective in the Holmesian mould. Christine, however, is resplendently bespoke, in a smart black tailored jacket and matching trousers pulled, as one sees from peering underneath the table, half-way up her shins, and elegant white bootees and socks. Her face is very white, her lips are red, her eyes I recall had a depth of blue the picture gives no notion of, and her hair, which is a darkish gold though in a natural light it had a whitish sheen, is not that of a ten-year-old but rather of an assured and stylish woman. I have always liked to have such women sitting next to me, whether they are blondes, brunettes or neither, as a form of reassurance, and Christine functioned as an early prototype. The other boy, whose name was Jones, is wearing a top hat and has a thick and opulent black beard, which he is firmly clinging on to, while from within his dark and baggy suit a crumpled shirt comes tumbling out. The plot being long forgotten, it seems most likely Christine was the heroine and I the hero of this drama, and Jones the dishevelled villain.

Christine aroused in me emotional feelings which Jones was also subject to, and together we took part in an adventure that contained some hidden rivalry, though without him I would not have dared to undertake it. Christine, we had got to know, was living further down the road to which the church had given its identity. We had also, by some means or other also now forgotten, found out the number of her house and had arranged to meet when darkness was already falling and the world retiring into night. And thus it was we gathered, illuminated only by the street lamps, like plotters in a Shakespeare tragedy, and at once set off, primed with our inside information. We stood, it seemed precariously, on the far side of the road but in the shadow of the pavement, from which we could observe the bedroom window, its curtains still wide open for our furtive conning of an interior brightly lit, wherein Christine, looking straight in front of her as if into a mirror which was well above our heads, was seated on a bedroom chair, and over her was bent her mother in the part of an assiduous coiffeuse, brushing and combing through the long waves of her tresses with the unchanging iteration of the sea.

For me this little episode had all the pleasure and anxiety of its insecurity, and having made our amorous point, which was the full extent of our devotion, we faded on the blowing of a horn.

Coincidence may be notable for incongruity. Many years after this adventure the translated school would look across at what had once been Christine's window from just behind the very spot which we had stood on in our separate raptures.

In my final year I gained admission to a secondary school where I would very soon become a boarder. The concomitant was my separation – as it proved, for ever – from my family. My mother had gone with me to this school and waited elsewhere while I had two interviews, or tests. One, with the Headmaster, had to do with reading skills and comprehension, whereas the other seemed to be a test of memory. The first was held in an imposing study, with comfortable furniture and lamps so soft in their effects their purpose might have been to see if you could keep awake, which my anxiety ensured. I walked across a carpet into which, with each irresolute step, my shoes began to sink. It had an unfamiliar plushness which disarmed me. Behind his gleaming desk awaited the Headmaster, his hair immaculately silver, his tall figure consummately upright, his manner graciously impeccable. He asked me to read a passage from a book he gave me, which I hoped I had got through to his satisfaction. But now I found he had a question. Did I think the man about whom I had just been reading wise or foolish? My mind had been on reading rather than on the meaning, which I had gleaned as it were in passing rather than by any close attention, and on this flimsy ground I ventured that I thought him foolish, which I took from his benignant smile, followed at once by my dismissal, to have been the wiser answer.

I was escorted to another building for a meeting with his Deputy, and was shown into a very dark and very narrow room whose glimmers, which were the only proof that it was late on in the morning, descended from a skylight far above. I was in what appeared to be a widened corridor, which left no margin either for the Deputy behind his empty table or for his victim on its other side. Meanwhile its length extended from the door I had come in at to the place where I was sitting and beyond this to the obscurities of the place's further reaches. If this table had a function in proceedings it could only have been to make one lose one's bearings.

The Deputy was short and bald and very round but not in the slightest jolly. He seemed to have dispensed with the preliminaries as interfering with his duties. He read, from a paper he was holding that I couldn't see, a random set of numbers going from 1 to 9, which I found I must at once say back to him, to begin with in the order

I had heard them but then, which was much harder, with a quite different set of numbers, backwards. Each time I gave my answer he increased – by one – the total, as in the gradual tightening of a rack. But finally he signified that he had done with me and I could go, which I might take to mean that I could go no further than I had.

In the light of my admission to this school my father took a step for which I have to thank him. It was an act of foresight which, I was to find, gave me an advantage over many of my fellow pupils. In my final summer term at primary school I had to go one afternoon each week, when school was over, to a Latin tutor. This tutor was the very Mr Wakefield who had so publicly undermined me. I'd said nothing, however, in the meanwhile to disturb my father's trust in him, being certain that my father who, stern in most matters, remained inflexibly a northerner, would have been unable not to feel aggrieved at Mr Wakefield if he had known about his bias. The two years that had succeeded had let the memory fade. I had seen little of Mr Wakefield during them, and such encounters as we had were not important. Besides, it was a memory of the kind one stifles. My mind was less on that than on the double challenge of the journey and the Latin language. Having received directions to the town where Mr Wakefield lived, I had to trust now to my sharpness, the roads I was to go along, as also the type of vehicle I was to travel in, being quite unknown to me.

This vehicle was what was called a trolley bus, for reasons I supposed connected with the means of its propulsion, in which a pole diagonally linked up with a wire running up above it. It was, among all the London Transport buses – single- and double-deckers, most of them red but some, because they went into the country, green – in my own mind an anomaly. And it made its own mark on my weekly journey in the anonymous built-up roads of urban Surrey. At first the journey's interest lay in my anxiety not to miss the stop where I got off, especially as the route had in it many bends and junctions all so very like each other. This stop was not far distant from a traffic lights and crossroads in another Surrey town. I had a fear of being lost and another, linked with it, of being late. (Even today so many of my troubling dreams concern my being in a town I cease to recognise and am unable to negotiate and which, as I am struggling, alters all its roads and buildings, its elevation and configuration, so that what had once been level streets become steep hills, or else removes the trains or buses I must catch, or deconstructs the bus stops and the people waiting at them, so that at the climax, as the light is failing, I have lost all touch with where I am or how I might find where I should be.) With routine, however, came a feeling of familiarity and ever fewer glances through the window at our progress. Even the nature of our turns at corners or our stops at traffic lights could be relied on to inform me, although I felt the need still to look up.

Mr Wakefield's flat was almost just above the traffic lights I had got off at and partly overlooked them from its first floor window, so that as I sat with him and Mrs Wakefield having tea before the trial that would follow, not this time of my spoken English but my Latin, I could almost see the bus stop where, within the hour, I would regain my freedom. Before this moment came, another would precede it when I had to leave the table and walk over to a smaller one at which, in a supportive armchair, I was confronted by the Latin language. Here, with Mr Wakefield, I encountered Ancient Europe, progressing thence to Ancient Rome; then a Roman Girl was introduced, succeeded by a Roman Lady and her Daughter. In the midst of these, there were encounters also with vocabulary and grammar, and conjugations and declensions, and also a first encounter with pronunciation, where I gathered that each vowel had two sounds depending on its being long or short, so that a long "a" was pronounced as in the English "father", a short one as in the English "fat". I made no link of any kind on learning this with Mr Wakefield's first dismay on meeting me. Nor did I think, until I was much older, of the irregularities in received pronunciation of the letter "a" or of the growth historically of the ascendancy and cultural bias of the south of England, which ever since has stayed in place.

My weekdays, from setting off for school until the early evening, when the door would open and my father would come in to greet my mother, were times of comfort and stability. They had a pattern that was even and agreeable; they had in them friends and pleasures, and they offered me two freedoms: a freedom of movement coming home, and a freedom from being criticised. These middle hours of the day were moments lacking tension, and I think back on them as if they had always taken place in sunshine.

My father's anger, I had long discovered, was never far away, but ready always to be sparked by failure to comply with his required procedures. For me the breakfast, lunch or supper table was a dangerous environment, and especially at weekends I would approach it with unease, in a spirit of premonition. I had learned there were innumerable unsuspected ways to stoke his fury. Nothing was likelier than forfeiture of his approval. My offences might be of a sort to have me sent to bed or to cause me to be beaten. This, to spare my mother, he would conduct beyond her hearing in my bedroom, whose role as a place of refuge would be, not only by his actions but his presence, sullied. I was left to argue with myself about my guilt or innocence and correspondingly my father's rationale. My mother would be distressed – I liked to think on my behalf – but, faithful to her husband, invariably supported him, if only tacitly, not only because he was her husband but because he had his legislative duty as male parent, a role which like a judge's tolerates no challenge. Once, though, at a weekend, she displayed her mercy when a bowl of bread and butter pudding that had caused me nausea had continued as my menu for the breakfast, lunch and supper following. When the next morning my father had departed for his train, my mother silently removed the bowl and nothing more was said about it. Perhaps, if later he raised questions, she may have claimed that I had eaten it, or urged that I had had sufficient punishment, or that she couldn't let me go to school not having had my breakfast. Austerity, however, was a mode well suited to my father's nature. Nausea was unmentioned in his medical encyclopaedia, and if encountered was to be resisted. It was a moral not aesthetic question and as well a matter of his authority. Such indulgences as my mother showed me fostered the assumption that her love for me was surely absolute. And this illusion I still believed in, and which sustained me through my unhappiness with my father, I was able to maintain even when not much later, when I no longer lived with them but was at boarding school and they in the Sudan, my mother offered me, when finally I could go to see her, the order of her priorities, in which a husband naturally had the precedence, a child being merely secondary. She said it with the sobriety of one who quotes not only her personal feelings but the established moral order. This circumscription of her duties and emotions was beyond my understanding or imagination, and a limit on our relationship that I could only, for my own good, disregard. And yet, as her honest and indeed uncompromising statement of the case, it couldn't be forgotten and was the beginning of my journey into disillusionment.

CHAPTER V

I LEAVE HOME

Fear is suffering over what is coming certainly or potentially, whether imminently or further off. I had spent the end of 1952 in fear of January, 1953, whose alteration to my circumstances was to be both soon and certain.

My father was about to take up his command in the Sudan. My family life, I had to grasp, was over. On a cold, grey, rainless day, early in that fateful month, a taxi pulled up at the gate. My mother, standing behind a curtain as if to camouflage her anguish, dabbed at eyes too full, however, of knowledge, as, my father striding out ahead, I set off down the brutal shortness of the garden path. I looked back for a final glimpse of her, but she had disappeared already in the dark reflections of the glass through which, though already irretrievable, she might still be watching me.

As he approached the gate my father greeted Mr Stead, who was to drive us into London, with a remark about the cold which he would soon have put behind him.   I followed him through the gate on to the pavement, where Mr Stead relieved me of my case and put it in the boot before returning to his seat. I sat, as instructed, in the back, whereas my father sat in front with Mr Stead, not only to be sociable but, as he said, to help him with the route, though Mr Stead assured him that he knew it. His tone was both respectful and, as his name had intimated, steady. He may also have been a kindly man who, without so much as saying so, and knowing the purpose of the journey, was thinking it might be more agreeable for us if my father were to sit beside me in the back.

The car was put in gear, and as it pulled away I looked out through the glass, seeking to make some final contact with the house I had called my home. But its expression was impassive. For it there was no disruption. It was not a house inclined to share one's feelings, whereas other houses I have lived or even merely stayed in have displayed an empathy beyond the reach, I have learned to see, of many of my fellow human beings with whom ostensibly I have had a near connection.

In only a moment we had turned the corner, and all my past life in that house and street, suddenly become so vital, was obliterated. For a while I watched go by the buildings, trees and hedges that I knew so well and had taken always for granted, but which now assumed a dearness for me they could not have had if I had not been leaving them. And soon we had moved beyond them to a strange new territory whose roads were busy main ones and surroundings unfamiliar and indifferent, and I withdrew into a resignation which, instead of offering numbness, was obliged to struggle with my turmoil.

We were coming down a little hill with trees and green beside it. And then we stopped. It was a toll gate we had arrived at. We were very nearly there. My father spoke curtly to Mr Stead, and from where I sat behind I saw the coldness in his pale blue eyes of which I had myself so often been the object. Mr Stead, it seemed, had taken a wrong turning, although we were in the very College road which was to be my home for longer than my heart would let me think of. There was threepence to be paid before we could proceed, which Mr Stead was handing to the gate man and would be added to the fare. My father, whom the increase much annoyed, withdrew his angry gaze from Mr Stead and fixed it on the narrow view outside his window, while meanwhile Mr Stead drove on, it felt to me, uncomfortably. We approached and passed the school's imperious central buildings – their heights and symmetries, their pinnacles and chimneys, tower and spire, their brick that was faced with stone, their contemporaneity with Empire – and then went over an arterial road, and then sedately on again with large Edwardian houses on each side hiding behind their walls and hedges, until, as we were going down a gentle slope which seemed as if it might have wished to give me comfort, we turned into a curving gravel drive beside which was the wide and imperturbable Georgian building now to become my home and, as time would make apparent, the possessor of a multitude of secrets guarded by it with immaculate discretion.

It was too early in the afternoon for any other boys to be there. It was the housemaster who greeted us. He was a tall, large, stooping man with wary bloodshot eyes that seemed to have shrunk back in their sockets. His smile was a movement that, having begun to raise his cheeks, left them to fall as suddenly, and the humanity which I would learn much later he possessed, though as if it were a secret not to be too readily uncovered, failed to disturb the gruff notes of his vocal chords. He took us through his hall and through a door and down a narrow passage. There was an opening on the right through which he led us and then stopped. I gazed into a dormitory, where my eyes at once took in the lines of beds along each wall. Among them, however, were some windows, through which a lawn and old brick wall and trees appeared to soften the impression, while nearer at hand inside the door the bed prescribed for me attended in its corner. I stood my case beside it.

Meanwhile my father had been drawn aside into the corridor. I took it they were discussing me regarding the arrangements and anything else about me needing saying, a matter privy to them, and so I waited out of hearing. Very soon, however, my father reappeared and, by way of a summation, noted that we would meet again in three years' time. To this plain statement of the matter I responded with appropriate sangfroid, at which he shook my hand in brisk and military style, withdrew into the corridor and vanished. It was with an empty kind of anguish that I imagined him rejoining Mr Stead, who by another route would take him home again, his business as it had to do with me concluded to his satisfaction.

Soon afterwards the housemaster, glancing in at me through the doorway, which, I would come to find, although there was a door fixed back against the wall, was always open in the greater interests of surveillance, told me to wait there for the matron, and then he also disappeared. After a while I went into the corridor and came upon a large room furnished with long tables and wooden chairs placed up against them. There was no one there. I returned into the dormitory and stood, waiting, by my bed. It was the beginning of my life alone.

CHAPTER VI

NIGHT DREAMS

Links between people in which their feelings have been positively charged may well come through what seems to be a final rupture. While contact may be lost through separation not for a short time but for years on end, and it seems that our affection or attraction, whatever good or bad there might have been in it, is irretrievable, these links are not like brittle metal links but akin to winter bulbs, awaiting hardily and determinedly their warming moment. Though our link may have been muted, lacking a voice and an expression, and it might appear forgotten, it may choose to show itself in dreams, confronting us with our regrets and longings.

What happened, I suppose, with Pauline was that soon afterwards I set off with my family to our new life on London's borders but in Surrey, which some years after we had left it was deemed to be in London after all. Thought of the north soon faded, and Pauline with it. A few years passed: room enough for her erasure, that proved after all delusory, to have started and be about to finish. Now I was twelve years old, at school in London, my family far off in Sudan. It must be a fault of memory that I don't recall within those years in Surrey, which seem now as if they had begun and ended gummed down in an envelope, a single thought of Pauline. It was as if she had been struck through like a word misplaced in a sentence.

I was, or felt, alone now in the world. In the holidays my mother's younger sister, Shirley, had no option but to stand in for my mother, though she addressed the matter in good spirit and I suspect with some compassion. She had at her side her husband, Laurence or, as everyone called him, Laurie, a gentle, unassuming man who grasped the subtlety of his commission, his exercise of an authority he didn't claim or doubtless want being indeed so muted as to come out of him apologetically, whereas the respect I sensed in him for how I had to stand in things was, without my telling him I thought this, something that upheld me.

He was an accomplished amateur photographer, a knowledgeable "railway buff", and passionate observer and recorder of steam railway engines and the multiplicity of their parts. He was an honest, law-abiding man who trespassed on the railways for his photographs; I, by his side, nervous less of the imminence of the locomotives than of their approaching drivers and their firemen and the powers of the authorities, was fortified by my companion's presence.

Sometimes we cycled out through Harrogate, and then through Knaresborough and Boroughbridge into the nether country of small lanes and villages belonging to the Vale of York, until we were in a world where, other than our tyres' swishing murmur, there was no sign or sound of life, and this too ceased as we dismounted, making the silence audible. Now, over a fence and down a bank, we stood beside the railway lines. Some distance off there was a signal box in which I was conscious there must be a signalman who might have sight of us and who, after long pauses, suddenly and unpredictably, with an abrupt click, would change the points and signals. The lines stretched either way into a trembling glimmer. For we were standing at the heart of eighteen straight and level miles in which, from London or from Edinburgh, expresses of the first importance, appearing far off as a shapeless blur but mutating as they drew nearer into an identity, finally scorched by us, shuddering as if in agony unless it were in ecstasy. My main interest was in the class of locomotive, which would almost certainly be a Pacific, even perhaps what most would please me, which was also the most elusive, an A4, its moulded curves in blue or green or even silver livery, although the last of these I never had the luck to see. Or from further up or down the line a goods train might more ponderously come round towards us from the east, its driver or its fireman, according to the way that it was going, glancing over at us as it laboured by.

By means which yet again I don't recall, it was arranged for me to spend some days with Pauline, now resident in Sheffield with a man who may or mayn't have been her husband. I had just turned twelve, while Pauline would by now have got perhaps to twenty-one. Did Pauline know I was in Yorkshire, staying with my aunt, and if so, how? What agency informed her? Was it my mother in a letter from Khartoum, or was it Shirley closer by in Harrogate? Was Pauline asked if she would like to have me? Was I asked if I would like to stay with her? What seems unlikely is that, out of the depths whether of my forgetting or remembering her, the impulse would have come from me. It seems unlikely too that Pauline would have been in contact with my aunt, and even more unlikely that my aunt, who disapproved of her, would have encouraged Pauline; all which leaves me to wonder if the agents of our reunion might more probably have been our mothers, who had looked fondly from my life's beginning on my love for Pauline and on hers for me.

I was becoming more relaxed on journeys. I would travel third class on the Pullman, from a platform at King's Cross which was always reassuringly the same to another at my destination, Harrogate, which was similarly invariable, but when I was returning differed and in that difference was consistently the same. It wasn't therefore long before I had the easy manner of a seasoned passenger and hardened veteran of these stations and their platforms for which there grew in me a kind of love, whether the rapture of a lover who once more greets his freedom with his mistress, or the sorrowing adieu of one who must return from her to prison.

Now I set off, accompanied by my case, to Sheffield. Arriving at its station, whose stone these days is whitish brown but would then have been much blacker, I proceeded in an uncertain spirit to the entrance hall, where among all the people waiting I saw her instantly; for her looks that over time had grown elusive reappeared as if I had always had them with me, and it was only that I'd temporarily mislaid them. I walked towards her overcome and diffident. She wasn't, however, by herself. By the side of her stood a tall young man with little waves of red-brown hair and an expression that thereafter stayed in place, demonstrating its obscure amusement and a tolerance of my being there which seemed perhaps conditional.

We walked out to his little sports car painted red. I found I was to sit on Pauline's lap, with which Norman said he understood I'd had some previous contact, and in any case it was the only place for me to sit unless I squeezed myself between them.

'He means,' she said, with a reproving glance at him, 'when you were little, when you were a baby.'

And so I settled on her lap, my feelings, however, in confusion, which perhaps she sensed, for at once she leant down to my cheek beneath her, dwelling on it with a kiss which like a syrup seemed to ooze all through me;

though already, when I had felt her pressure in the station, she had given me what I longed for, which was reassurance. She had on a lilac summer frock with straps up to her shoulders, giving my eyes a view of her they couldn't not keep coming back to as to their point of rest. I knew, though, that she was watching me, but told myself it was indulgently, it was what she had intended I should do, that not to look at her would be not only difficult but hurtful. Did I recognise an unconfessed complicity between us, that in our minds there was a hardly buried memory which was taking strength from our behaviour?

She said we were having fish and chips for supper, which she hoped I didn't mind, and I said there could be nothing I liked better or more suitable for a Friday, though why this was I was uncertain and in any case she quite ignored. We went into the fish and chip shop, where we stood together in the queue while Norman waited in his car. It was as if we were alone there in a past excluding Norman. I was afraid he didn't care for me or for my presence and wondered what he knew or mightn't know about me or what impression she had given him of how she saw or thought of me. And I kept returning to the question of our night together all those years before and how she had regarded it and how she still regarded it and whether, because I didn't know what she was thinking, she had ever thought about it in the meantime. With a view to reinforcing our connection, I said it was a strange coincidence we were in Sheffield, a place I had never been to in my life till then, because it was to Sheffield she had been going when I had stayed with her and Auntie Win. But to this also, perhaps because it was quite obvious or because her mind had things in it she didn't wish to share with me, she only answered, as a gap had opened just in front of us, that we needed to move up a little.

I trusted, however, in her affection. In spite of having seen so very little of her I had always been in others' eyes her favourite, and was confident still she liked me, which her behaviour had already proved, though I was also conscious, meeting her again, how vulnerable she made me feel, being so unlike me and perhaps in fact unreachable. And when suddenly our eyes were for a moment on each other and she failed to look away I was aware of blushing, and knowing this blushed only the more intensely, which is what will happen when women who are aware they are attractive practise on us, like musicians on their instruments, with the nuances of their expression.

She asked me about my school and wondered if I found it daunting. She was sure she would have done, especially its lack of freedom. I said, measuring my answer, that I was growing better used to it and that my being there, I knew, was in my interests. I avoided calling on her sympathies, fearing that, while she might feel sorry for me, she might also begin to think me weak, whereas my hope was to appear mature. She thought it quite extraordinary and impressive that I was learning

Latin and wished sometimes she had learnt some French. Norman had promised to take her, although that day was long in coming, to Paris and Montmartre, which I took to be two separate places. My antipathy to Norman, which was growing keener, perhaps came basically from jealousy, and especially I resented his propensity to show me, by the familiarities he engaged in with her, who was 'master'. And I regretted her enjoyment of them, and wished she had concealed it from me. I felt there was something I wasn't sure of in her that caused her to play him off against me. In this I may have been affected by my aunt, who had felt unable not to offer me a word or two of her reserve concerning Pauline and the sort of people she was known to go about with. As for Norman, she had never met him but she knew enough from others to have made her judgement, whose adverse nature she left for me to realise.

He did me, however, what appeared a favour, by taking me with Pauline to both Hillsborough and Bramall Lane, where two north London teams were beaten on a Saturday and Monday. My pleasure was, though, mixed with disappointment. Arriving late on each occasion, we stood in the only place you could do, at the back, my situation worsening further on the Monday, when we were squeezed into the side of the pavilion, from which one's eyes traversed the empty cricket field to reach eventually the distant football pitch, now in the evening gloom a fading shadow of itself. This was, however, less a problem than my being hidden down below, from which I could follow only moments when the ball flew high up in the air before it disappeared again behind the man in front of me, whereas Norman's head rose up above all others, his eyes surmounting all impediments while I stood gazing at the backs and taking in the roars of those denying me a view. He gave no indication that he favoured either Sheffield team. He was a Sheffield boy and wasn't partisan it seemed about its parts.

Norman I would much rather, I found, have done without, a view I feared he took of me. There was, I soon discovered, an unbridgeable divide between us. Firstly, as I have said, there was the jealousy I felt towards him, which was aggravated by the way he flaunted his possession of her. And clearly he resented my long standing with her that went as far back as it could do, to my birth. We were even relations of a kind, if only through her adoption. I felt he didn't like the way she talked to me, which from his own perspective might have seemed too knowing, for her acuteness seized upon my private feelings. Such warmth and curiosity, in which there was a certain prurience, I was unused to. I couldn't know how well aware or not she was of Norman's feelings of discomfort at her manner with me, which she carried off so naturally and, it might have seemed, unconsciously, as with someone she had long been close to, which in a sense was true but also false.

Beside my gap in age with Norman there was as well a social gulf, accentuated by our prejudices. Wasn't he a local boy who, for all I knew or could detect, had been given no particular advantages and by a certain showiness or sharpness had created in himself what the people I now lived among, within the guarded boundaries of a school like mine, would have observed without enthusiasm? They might have seen in him the very type which was to them anathema. And how did he see me? As someone he might well suspect regarded him with condescension and even perhaps despised him secretly? As having opted, socially, for a journey of dissociation? Whose head was filling up with Latinist superiority and privilege? And perhaps my having come from north of him in Yorkshire only fuelled his antipathy. Perhaps, despite the closeness that I had with Pauline, a part of him struck out my Yorkshire past as if I had invented it, whereas the other part acknowledged it and damned me as a fake. I was not that but a person who already knew the need I had to fit in with the world in which I largely found myself.

Yet, when everything had been said about our mutual suspicion, Norman was her lover and her keeper and I a pubescent boy remote from her in time and place. My stay was after all a very short one which he'd make sure was not repeated. Our common aim was to give each other nothing in the way of credit. He was absurdly jealous of a boy of twelve and I absurdly jealous of her partner. And Pauline would have observed this with a clutch of feelings that would have had in them the satisfaction of a woman well familiar with her powers over men as well as a tender understanding of her lover's insecurity with me and mine with him, in which she saw these powers working.

My last evening with Pauline had arrived, and though I was only going back to Harrogate and not as yet to London, I felt that loss or that anxiety which all through life has joined me in departures. As it was Monday, supper drew on what was left unfinished. And so we had sharp cuts of beef sliced off the joint by Norman's carving knife, an instrument he wielded like a rapier, with tenacious thrusts. He informed me I must learn the art, for until you had it you were not a man. This was the moment when it struck me who it was, though so unlike him, he made me think of, which was a further reason for my feeling ill at ease when I was near him. For my father too carved beef, though without his ostentatious flourish, achieving his more sober pleasure in a grim and reverential manner from which one should deduce this was no matter to be undertaken unadvisedly or lightly, but reverently and discreetly, being in fact of the order of a ritual and devotion; he was in all my knowledge of him a devout attender at whichever church he happened to be nearest to, providing that while it was not too low it was also not too high (to which All Saints had risen ecumenically dangerously near). This unlikely similarity to my father, which made me look at him more closely, at once produced another, which was the similarity of their moustaches: of military shortness and clipped as if by slide rule, Norman's was, however, different in its colour, being a reddish-brown whereas my father's was a tawny shade of yellow; and Norman's eyes, fixed now on the slice he was addressing, were of the same pale greyish-blue, so pale indeed you might have mixed them up with watercolours that had been too heavily diluted.

There was a further thing, in Norman's view, I must get down me to become a proper man, which man's drink he put before me in the kind of plain glass utilised by publicans. Through it, in steady order, bubbles rose. My father had preceded him in this initiation rite one Sunday when as usual we were solemnising lunch.

My first sip instantly confirmed my apprehensions. The taste recalled my father's bitter India ale, which at our severe and much feared lunches was a core ingredient of his piety. Norman, though, insisted that I drink it, following his example, like a man, and so I did, knowing the greater pain of failure, with more however to come when I had drained it and had begun to feel that there had entered into his sardonic smile the embryo of his approval.

Warmed perhaps by this rapprochement, Pauline now confided they were "night birds". They knew Sheffield in the dark, she thought, rather better than in the light. The clubs, to which naturally they couldn't take me, though Pauline said she would have loved to tack them to my London education, were she could say a kind of home from home for them. Norman, she acknowledged, was if he was anything a spender, and she looked at him approvingly yet disapprovingly, provoking him to look at me and then at her as if to ask what was his better option. They didn't live, she didn't suppose, the kind of lives my low church aunt would have approved of. I took this as inviting me to slight my aunt, to whom I was indebted; but by not maligning her I risked dissatisfying Pauline. And so I fixed instead on her denomination and said she was a Methodist, as was in fact her husband, who was also a lay preacher, which Norman said could not have better made the point that Pauline had been getting at.

*

I woke up in a dark that was intense. Neither Orion nor the moon could pierce my shroud of curtains. At once I knew the reason for my waking, which in those unfledged days was not the habit it became in later years when time was taking hold of me. I reached out for the lamp switch. My watch informed me it was nearly three o'clock. Hurrying to the landing, which was a long one and in darkness, I began to feel my way along it. The bathroom was at the end, far off, beyond the stairs, its door in front of me. At once I noticed something glowing round it, not in the diffused manner of a halo but in thin, sharp lines, like a gilt frame round a canvas. It was possible they had left the light on for some reason.

Or else there was someone in there. I stood, not knowing what to do, yet certain what I must do. Suddenly I heard a vibrant laugh from Pauline and then a lower, man's tone. I had them both to face together. Now I had reached the door. I was afraid to knock but dared to turn the knob, as if this latter act would not be so invasive. No sooner had I touched it than the door itself, not having been quite closed, began to swing a little inward, creaking. Pauline at once called out to ask if it was me, and though her voice was gentle and, I told myself, inviting, I was unable to reply. Instead I pushed the door a little further so that about a half of me appeared, but subject to the light's hard glare.

The bathroom was a square and large one, and at its centre was the bath, positioned horizontally to the door and at an angle from it to the right. Across the floor's bare boards I faced them both. In the bath was Pauline, sitting at its further end. She smiled the moment that she saw me, in a welcome by which she seemed to bring me in. Stationed behind her and the bath, in dinner jacket and bow tie, the latter's flamboyant scarlet matching, as if borrowed from her gloss, the lustrous redness of her lips, Norman stood immobile and remote, as if to disregard me. It was a woman I was looking at whom I had seen before, but very long before, the only woman I had ever seen in such a guise, but now at another sharper angle from which her salient aspects, rounded, upright, addressed me with a dilemma, moral and aesthetic, whose contraries were immobilising. As, still, I hesitated, she rose up, a contemporary Venus from the sea, the streams of water that had bathed her shining on her undulations and, which my eyes could only hide away from yet immediately returned to, the drenched forest glistening and dripping at her centre. What may have been, that moment, in her mind remains for me forever an obscurity. Was it that she was generous or cruel, tender or indifferent, or playing with her lover, or an exhibitionist? Confused and overcome, I turned away and, pulling the door shut as I did so, fled.

Lying again in bed, I found the sources of my comfort and discomfort had changed places. It seemed my mental turbulence had anaesthetised my body. I fell asleep at last, my eyes in thrall to her.

I awoke early in a sink of horror. I longed for it not to be so – an eradication well beyond my power. All I could hope for was concealment until I too was hidden in the train. Wasn't I innocent – yet guilty? My caring so greatly how she thought of me intensified my shame. I feared her disillusionment, the forfeit of her affection. And in that agony I quit her at the station.

I have no memory of writing to her afterwards, or of my aunt inquiring whether I had done so, an inquiry she may well have thought belonged within her duty. All of those details vanished long ago. I can, however, imagine now the conflict there would have been in me between the need to write a letter thanking her and on the other hand the fear that would have caused me not to, not wishing to impose myself, not even on a piece of paper. What then could I require of her? What I longed for was compassion and exoneration, which might after all be best expressed by silence, though silence lends itself to ambiguity – the anguish of uncertainty. But this longing to be reassured and given comfort was to be frustrated. Whatever she now thought of me was something she withheld, for I never heard from her again. Even within the raw emancipation of our times the places of our sexuality are still, as they have always been, our guilty secrets.

PART TWO

CHAPTER VII

GOING OUT

It was a crossroads with two spurs, so that six roads entered or departed from it. Four made up the cross and the two lesser, which were more lanes than roads, inserted a diagonal. The slanting angle of these two, being less urgent, added to the friendly natures given them by their gentler traffic; for the road that disappeared into a bit of country and eventually wound back among the door-steps and the chimneys was the least used of them all and also on the further side from us, while across from it our own road sauntered in its easy-going manner upwards to the cobbled square.

I say "our road", though the nearest was the main road, indifferent to us, that hurried past our lowly turning. We were a short way down a little cinder track beside which stood the plain brick backs of houses and their small untidy yards of worn-down grass. To venture to that road meant entering a dangerous world in which high-handed overbearing vans and hard uncompromising lorries thundered past the narrow

97

pavement that we had to walk on. The road, though our neighbour, was not a being we felt kin to. A short way from our gate, it had the rumble of artillery. Yet in those long past times a small child might be trusted with unusual freedom.

Confronting the cheap brick faces of our houses rose a high stone wall beyond which in the summer nothing except the branches of some trees was visible, though when the wind was blowing a mysterious grey roof came in and out of view. But in winter it laid bare its slated pitches, which were always saturnine. It came over as a building of some grandeur, with owners who, being never seen or spoken of, remained mysterious. Between the wall and avenue along which only carts and downcast little horses ventured there was a bank of earth where, in the summer, canes and brambles jostled for ascendancy and in the winter falling snow presided.

The avenue – it had that name – possessed two characters. The back was its utilitarian and common self. The front gazed out more comfortably from its pale brown stone, made up of narrow shapely pieces – blackened, however, randomly by soot they had, over so many smoky years, acquired. As the more desirable, this eastern side was less accessible. Here was the room with the piano, lace and drapes, the Scarborough water-colour in a dull gold frame, and the sofa and the armchairs which were not in general use, much like the guards' vans on the railways during their later obsolescence. It was a room which though at hand was out of reach, protected by its key and lock, secure behind its door. It was the holy place and refuge of my mother's mother, Edith.

There were, though, moments which disturbed its sleepy quarantine. There might be visitors for whom the room, exceptionally, was opened and tea was served in fine, bone china cups with sandwiches like wafers on plates as delicately thin. Yet the best china kept its station, untouchable in its cabinet whose beaded glass partitions, by severing handles or dissecting saucers in a dismemberment which never altered, seemed only to reinforce its fixity. Here beyond human reach were little Coalport cups and saucers with sprigs and stems in brown and shades of green on which were lodged pink buds in clusters and also separated single flowers with yellow centres in blue frames. And then there were the larger, shallower Chelsea cups and saucers, hand-painted with a blue wash base and core surmounted and encircled by a self-effacing white and yellow ground on which were horizontal sprays of leaves supporting red or violet petals. I write this not from memory but possession, these cups and saucers which had been her father's having been left me by my mother, who knew how I admired them.

But the times for me of more importance were when Edith took me in with her or had left the door ajar for me to join her as she sat at her piano, to the left side of the window where the shade was, and played with the finesse of one who had accompanied well known tenors

99

and sopranos at the city's concert hall. I would stand beside her listening to the three contrasting movements – the hushed adagio sostenuto, the briskly cheerful allegretto, the passionately demanding presto agitato – of the Sonata in C sharp minor, and to much other Beethoven and also Chopin, which she went on playing for some further years in which her hands became more crippled and, in the end, impediments and adversaries. It was entirely through her that I met and fell in love with serious music before I ever read a serious book or looked at serious paintings.

The window, whose equivalent in some other houses came forward in a bay, looked out upon the little lawn and hedge, beyond which was a path and then another hedge; then, as if it had been in London, in Knightsbridge or in Brompton (though nothing was more improbable), there was a garden which was for me a place of wonder, with a church's sanctity, only to be entered with an adult. It was long and narrow, with flower borders down the edges of a lawn just broad enough for two or three to walk together or, if it were warm and sunny, sit on. And from the angle of a baby's or a small child's gaze its beds in summer were a cultivated jungle from which roses, phlox and lupins, their heads up in the blue, dispensed – as from the heavens – nectar of an intensity from me long distant.

Beyond the further border came another hedge, and then a matching path to ours, and then another little line of hedges interspersed with wooden gates inside which were some pocket gardens much like ours. Rounding off the symmetry there was another line of houses, some in a terrace, and others in pairs or single, among which, further up beyond the road, there was a bungalow. Here, where great-aunt Amy lived, I first encountered the coincidence of pain and pleasure, pleasure arriving as an orange and pain in close attendance as a wasp. The old lady, though enfeebled, enjoyed more light and space than we at home did, with an outlook sweeping off beyond her garden to the great field just above, which climbed up by a final steeper gradient to the high street, the back views of its shops and other far off buildings blurred and indeterminate.

When, it must have been, I was five, and starting to remark things, I had a glimmer of an insight that fell perhaps within the architectural or sociological. It was an insight I kept hidden, not perhaps from a fear of showing it but merely as a private apprehension, a negative idea I accommodated, and perhaps because already I was distinguishing between what lay more naturally inside me and what might be communicated. What I had noted was the better circumstances of the buildings opposite, as was shown in some of their bow windows. They had a confident well-being that our own mere flat ones, in their modest two dimensions, lacked. And the contrast seemed to demonstrate a gap in human circumstances and even perhaps entitlements, although their owners were all people, barring my great-aunt, of whom I was completely ignorant. This quasi-moral hold of buildings extended to the corner house beside the road on our side, which a local doctor owned and which, bigger than the rest, was commensurately more imposing, though as it took up so much of the space available it was obliged to lack a garden and be squeezed inside its narrow yard.

There were three ways to the centre of the village. I am calling it a village, as it was named and thought of and for all I know still is, though it had as much the feeling of a town and was in possession of a disused station which announced this. A village typically might have a main or high street and some others tapering off and wandering soon enough into the country just beyond (though now likely to be encroached on by new housing). But my village was a wider network much of which embraced those hard outlines often to be found in towns – those unforgiving regimented grids whose only lustre shines out from the doorsteps whitened each early morning, before the world approaches them, by kneeling housewives in their uniforms of headscarves. The village's identity was composite, its mills and factories abutting country hills and pastures, its unremitting traffic bypassing the ends of empty back lanes whose only occupants might be a grazing horse perhaps or nibbling sheep or, in a trampled muddy corner, cows that glanced round at you as you paused before them and held you for a moment to their unimpressed inspection. It was a type of country which offered moments when, turning off a busy road into the quiet of a lane, you found, having only just set off along it, you were hearing not the fading roar and thunder of the traffic but a silence interrupted only by the static – which soon also you no longer heard although you were still hearing it – of trees and hedges twittering.

Our home was on the village boundary. Across the road the dour buildings, whose massed impassive tiers of windows alternated uniformly with begirding brick, obscured from view the dingy little stream that served them from behind. Not knowing of its being there, I could know nothing of its history or geography. I didn't know that it had come to its industrial Lethe from another purer world, that it was the very same unwary being that had started its existence further up the road on our side, among the woods and gardens of an elevated park, babbling without a forethought down its grassy hill until quite suddenly, as it skipped along behind a wall that hid away the traffic, it sank once more beneath the ground as earlier it had trickled from it.

Of the three ways to the market square the two acknowledged ones meant going to the road and turning left along the pavement. The more circuitous of these, which made you walk the whole way to the traffic lights, accompanied your every step with danger, and though each forward step was one step nearer safety it was no less the same step further from it. The pavement led beyond the avenue's two garden gates, whose low profiles shunned the world's attention, whereas for me, my head being at their level, they constituted staging

103

posts on an uneasy journey. Close up to them, my eyes took in their iron tracery, whose scrolls and coils seemed so intent on mirroring the foliage just beyond they might have been reflections of it. A few steps later came a glimpse into the facing row of houses, and then a view, more functional, of their backs, which like our own were of a raw and undistinguished brick, and after that you passed their little serviceable lane which duplicated ours, and finally an old stone wall which, lower than our own, defined their border less explicitly. On the other side there was the narrow entrance to an alley, a walled passage which opened up a shorter route whose perils were more shadowy and unknowable.

If you kept, though, to the road, there were perhaps two hundred yards still to the traffic lights. Shortly before you reached them, up some steps, was a tobacconist's and paper shop which was also a confectioner's and which, if alone, I entered in a wary manner but when Bill, my friend, was with me in a spirit of bravura. Neither of these opposing states had any noticeable impact on the owner, whose manner, certainly with us, was one of steadfast taciturnity. He was a large and tall man sticking out around his middle while retreating at the same time far back in his glasses, which only added, being also round, to the impression of his circularity. He wore, in keeping with his girth, wide braces, against which his capacious shirt, as he reached up to his shelves, kept straining like a sail blown out at sea. This was a matter in his presence for decorum but, once we were beyond his window and invisible, for the satirical inflation of our puny stomachs. And more heroically we toasted, opening our paper bags, the bravery of our going in and miracle of our emerging.

A short way from the shop arrived the traffic lights, where you turned into the lane that led up to the square. At that corner you had in front of you the terrors you were for now avoiding. This time you knew you didn't have to go across the lane, which widened just before the lights as if to raise its standing in the face of other roads that were, as it was not, arterial, arriving from far distances and going on to others just as distant, from towns and cities of some note to others just as consequential. If, though, you had to cross it to the temporary refuge of the narrow pavement opposite, you had to look, and do so all at once, in multiple directions at the vehicles bearing down on you at different speeds as was determined by the changing lights, themselves directed by the sudden motions up and down of their remote conductor. As a distraction for one's eyes there was, beyond the corner building just in front of you across the lane, the vastness of the one beyond the road behind it, which reared up with its filthy windows in implacable superiority, requiring double-decker buses to manoeuvre, swaying dangerously round it, as they kept within the narrow limits of their allocation, in right angles which constrained their struggles to turn left.

Yet industry no less than people comes and goes.

105

Long after the anxious moments when I stood there hesitantly many such buildings were obliged to come down thundering their anguish as they vanished into dust. Some were granted after-life on cellulose by lecturers in social history, who might be also amateur photographers, determined to preserve before too late the aesthetics of these erstwhile monuments to their creators, who had overlooked them, through so many generations, from their villas and their mansions on the ridges up above the noxious valley floors. The very mill that had so troubled me was brought down like the rest. Its space now, perhaps to compensate for all the years of its oppression, has settled in a penitential manner to its new role as a humble patch of grass.

CHAPTER VIII

UNCLE GEORGE'S TREAT

If having turned left at the corner you set off up the lane you would not have gone a great way on it when, on your own side of the road, you passed an old stone house with leaded windows at the front and steps up to the door. On either side of it were well clipped bushes, rounded at the top. A low wall and a hedge reached all the way along beside the pavement, and you entered through them by a central gate which led into a narrow strip of garden with a pocket lawn. It was a house that made you want to go inside it. Its air of comfort was inviting and because of that I saw it as beyond my reach. It wasn't the kind of place that I imagined I belonged in. And yet its owner and my mother, not that I ever wholly understood this, were first cousins: my mother's mother was my Uncle George's father's sister.

Immediately beyond the house and by its side there was an entrance going back behind it to a covered building which was the depot for the vans that came and went, their high sides painted in a brilliant bright green. Across their upper middles, in large capitals that, depending on the light, looked gold or yellow or gold-yellow, the owner's name was published. This name, GEORGE SYKES & SONS, was readily identified with Uncle George but will have had an older provenance beyond my knowledge (my reach into the family tree stretched barely further than my arms and legs). Beneath, in smaller capitals, appeared the nature of the business – bakers and confectioners, or terms to that effect – and under that the names of local towns and cities in the daily round, which had the scope of several railway lines still shared, when I was growing up, between LNER and LMS.

My uncle had two brothers, one older and one younger, who though they were also uncles had the impalpability of vague acquaintances: they were hardly 'there' enough to be avuncular. The elder was conveyed to me as someone of great means, which may have come from his involvement in the family business or from some other source entirely. Invisibility enhanced his mystery. He may have had two daughters – one Rhona, the other Beryl – and a wife called Edna. If not, the names belonged to other of my relations. Or Edna may have been the name of George's woman friend of many years whose hopes of him were never realised nor, as time would make apparent, ever could have been.

The younger brother, Jack, whom I recall as having been lean-bodied and sharp-featured, was judged to lack his brothers' ethic and was represented to me, when I was old enough to learn this, as having 'personal issues' with what was designated 'regular employment', which came, I learned, from his antipathy to tedium. Whatever truth was lodged in this, I tended to believe it for no better reasons than the sharpness of his features and that he bore the name of Jack, indicative to my mind of someone not quite serious, and also because the young are always flattered to be confided in by older people, the more so when the tenor of the revelation is to someone else's disadvantage. Gratitude invites credulity. Even so he had acquired a charming and attractive wife from Canada, a tall brunette, and she had given him a daughter, two years or more my elder, of whom perhaps, because her manner with me was invariably superior, I was to some degree in awe.

The depot's gloom and gauntness underlined its chill. Only the vans themselves could counteract this with their lustre and the heavy fumes of their exhausts. You went from here into the house up narrow steps cut into it between bare walls the starker for being whitewashed, and then around the edges of a room which lay in an invariable twilight dominated by a sombre faintly gleaming dining table, which would have been mahogany, until you came out at the house's junction by the front door and the central staircase, which, from its width and upward sweep, looked down on you, a small boy at the bottom, with a very natural hauteur.

There are certain rooms able to impress themselves

above all others by virtue of whatever it is about their personality. Memory tends to keep them present in us. The door across the hall, beyond the stairs, led into such a room, although in this case memory draws on very few encounters. It was a room to which admittance was exceptional, opening up to an extensive local family – distributed around the village and beyond – most notably on Christmas Day, in an event which, notwithstanding Mrs Joe and Mr Pumblechook, I recall as being in its benevolence Dickensian. My uncle was a kind, well-meaning man who had the means to offer what he did without requiring compensatory guilt or grateful humbleness.

It was a room of size and substance, well equipped to handle several generations and varieties of cousins, as well as those, who might be almost no less welcome, whose access came by marriage. Only missing were those of military age who lacked exemption. Among them was my father. And so this larger gathering, which if the men had been there might have been intimidating, enjoyed the soft diffusion of the female atmosphere that was my reassuring norm. The matriarch at George's party was his mother, Ada. She was of comfortable build. A certain roundness tends to put observers at their ease. And her ponderous movement was accommodating. Her son, by contrast, had a gaunt, diminished look, constructed from a long and narrow nose and a profile that retreated apologetically to a chin that was receding. His hair, however, though thinning, swept backwards with a jaunty flourish. His laugh, which was high in pitch, had the timbre of a neigh, as if acknowledging one's point ironically or quizzically.

From the room's ceiling hung a dazzling chandelier, while down below, on coffee tables and the grand piano, softer radiances came from table lamps. Further off, across the room, a fire blazed within a vast and open hearth surmounted by a mantel and a gilt rococo mirror keeping, or so it seemed, our whole assembly under its surveillance. The deep pile of the carpet was a resting place for oriental rugs whose geometric shapes and colours guarded chairs and sofas and the little tables by their sides. In the centre stretched a vaster, more imperious dining table sumptuously draped in linen, mounted on which were such unheard of glories of confectionery as were for me a culinary Book of Revelations: eclairs and pastries, iced cakes and meringues, jam tarts and chocolate biscuits, mince pies, Christmas cake and trifle, jelly and blancmange, as well as apples, oranges and peaches, and – by no means least – unprecedented sandwiches, whose rich fillings spilled out from their walls.

How though, at this distance from the 1940s' rigours, vouch for the bread's or cream's constituents? As the bread may not have been pure white but the grey I had always known, so equally the cream may not have been the product of a dairy but a greaseproof wrapper. Wonder is more possible for the unwitting. Perhaps, though, the bread was really white and the cream was

111

truly cream, a reparatory gift from George to all his stoic family? For by then it could have been the war had ended and the grip of rationing had been, though only temporarily and delusively, abated.

Near the dining table, in the room's centre, was the grand piano. On this, after tea or supper, Edith might have played some Chopin waltzes or mazurkas, but my mother's turn on the piano stool had possibly for some a more immediate appeal. If Edith's mastery derived from unforgiving practice and aesthetic sensibility, my mother's was the outcome of a pre-war social life and a facility for reproducing music she had only ever danced to. My mother's touch was light and easy, whereas Edith, whom from a young age her father had released from family business only however to attach eight hours a day to a piano stool, had been a virtuoso much called upon by Leeds Town Hall. Both mother and daughter had their forte with which they were each entirely and undoubtingly content.

Shrouded in his cloak and hood, his face's lower reaches tucked away beneath a beard that straggled, my uncle George presided in a chair adjacent to the tumbling mound of presents. He was Father Christmas not only figuratively but literally. For such as me he posed a tension: while fearful of his appearance one might no less be anxious to be called up for a present. And his voice was hardly one of this world but of distant snowy mountains whose only occupants were reindeer. For George, who was a lover of the arts, had drawn up from his larynx, very much against his natural pitch, the deep tones of a concert bass. And later, having missed unnoted this most interesting part of the proceedings, he presided once again among us in his pin-striped suit.

Further up past Uncle George the lane forked, joining the market square above to left and right. Keeping always to the right, you reached a turning right, along which on its left side was the village school, immediately followed by the playground and, down a short and sudden slope, a precipitous junction with the major road whose thunder roared so scaringly below. Here, when I was four, my mother brought me to begin my schooling. A short while after my arrival we were let into the playground for what, I gathered later, was "the break". And now I found myself, as I had never been as yet, alone with jostling, screaming larger boys and girls to whom I was invisible.

I had begun my life there on my own, a little early, in the summer, perhaps because it was agreed that I was "ready", or it may have been for quite another reason I was never told of. I was therefore not merely new but younger than the others. And all through school life I would be among the youngest, which was less the advantage it might seem, of "being ahead", than the impediment of my being, in more telling ways, "behind". Disregarded in that strident heaving mass whose volume was more piercing even than the main road's orchestra, and not yet having grasped or taken to the school's routine, I pushed through to a friendly gap

I saw between stone posts, which was up against the bottom corner of the school and also the exit to the street, and at once set off determinedly along the pavement. My departure was abetted by the elevation of the line of classroom windows I was passing, from which, so far below them, I was wholly hidden.

My Odyssean journey home, whether by navigation of the traffic lights or through the troubling passage, reversed whichever of the ways my mother might have brought me. My early reappearance was a matter firstly for astonishment and then my being summarily returned. My action, however, was a template for the future. I had begun, that first morning of my schooldays, the struggle persisting all through life between evasion and endurance: between the converse ills of fleeing and remaining.

I have no memory, other than of that false beginning, of my time at this first school. I have no further memory of my going to it or returning, no memory either of the teachers or the pupils, or of the classrooms or the hall. My time there was a short one, but made its laboured way through all the snows of 1947. In the summer we left our home for good and went off to a very different world and life.

My true school was the little terrace house and avenue, either the daily practicalities of the back, which was in effect the front, or the uncustomary privileges of the front, which was in effect the back. My first teachers were my grandmother and mother, aided by my aunt.

As well as music, on the piano or my mother's knee, there was the world of children's books with pictures. And so Art introduced itself. This atmosphere of safety during war would disappear soon after it, when insecurity, of which I had already demonstrated signs, would take paternal hold of me.

Indoors, the tiny kitchen's little range provided for our cooking and our heat, which served to emphasise the cold beyond, since elsewhere fires were very rarely lit, so they were often in a state of having been prepared with coal and sticks and paper but then, for days or even weeks, left unignited. This gave to a hearth a chilly look, whereas if it had been empty I might have felt a little warmer. But in the little room behind the kitchen I had my own domain, hidden away beneath a small round table that, being set back from the door, was out of the prevailing draught. It spent its days, except when we were eating at it, sheathed in a deep plum damask cloth that had on it, in certain lights, a sheen. This covering overflowed the table's surface, hanging suspended down to its extremities, from which emerged its fringes like the turrets – thin ones – of a castle upside down. Within, I was like Wemmick in his snug redoubt at Walworth, for while I lacked both moat and drawbridge I had a fortress of my own in which resided with me certain key companions.

Two of them are living with me still. The first is a coloured picture book about a young boy's friendship with a tiger, which ended like so many friendships in the arrival of a lady tiger and a little family of the tiger's own. The other is a bear a single year my junior, having been born on my first birthday with his features fully grown and faculties already working, though he has long since, somewhere in his middle age, when he was in the hands of others less attached or caring, lost an eye; yet the one still left to him considers me with an unsettling tender insight. And through time the muscles in his arms have withered, and his fur has worn away in places, and his leg displays a gash I must avert my eyes from. He is one of my best friends, though propped up over many years now in the corner of a window-sill, disregarded and no longer talked to, sometimes needing to be repositioned, having, it could have been for months, dropped down upon his patched-up feet or with his face into the sill, looking as if he'd given up through my neglect of him, his spirit broken by my infidelity.

In this minute accommodation lived four adults in a state, as I recall it, not of conflict and raised voices but of harmony. Perhaps the key to this was gender, for of those adults three were female – a late-middle-aged mother of a gentle disposition and two daughters in their twenties, one married, the other soon to be (both husband and fiancé being absent in the war). The remaining adult was my mother's father, some years older than his spouse, and beaten down by failure. Within the closeness of our little kitchen he sat always to the range's left side by the window, from which he could observe the dingy patch of garden with its unkempt grass, beyond which was our garden wall, and after that, beyond the largely hidden avenue, the further higher wall, and finally some branches up above it and breaking through them particles of sky. His morning's pleasure was to watch the sparrows and his other breakfast customers. He was a man who once had run a colliery but had been ruined in the 1930s, and now sought only to be lost to view. As there was no fire in him, this patriarch who once had been respected, and was respected still although more greatly pitied by his wife and daughters, he had been put to be no bother to them in a corner.

This being my environment, I began life in a world whose warmth of feeling overcame its deprivation. My social life outside the family was a narrow one, amounting just to Bill, a name that, because of him, I have always liked to see as reassuring, though it has sometimes disappointed me. His house was further on towards the field that climbed, more steeply at its upper end, towards the main street of the village. Besides the doctor's daughter, called Virginia[5], whose corner house faced partly to the road, I don't recall there being any other child along our lane, although of course there may have been, perhaps too old or young for me to be aware of. Memory in my own case has seemed always most responsive to those fleeting moments of intensity which on their arrival bring surprise; or, by contrast, to the drill

[5] The name is illustrative of the long reach of coincidence.

of repetition, the staple fare of grammar teachers or the military parade ground.

Life has put in front of me three different kinds of friends. Of one of these Bill was the first. His type has proved uncommon, in the way of certain blood groups. He was my junior, though not by much, and shorter, with a thinner face than mine, and over his pink cheeks, which had a needy air, his eyes conveyed his diffidence. He made a good fit with my temperament, although our friendship was misleading, for the world, I was to find, was not as like him as might have better suited me. He didn't make me nervous or uncomfortable. With him I was, if either of us was, the leader, the one putting forward his ideas. Time, though, would show me that in Bill I had a prototype which, however well designed, would fail to enter mass production. It was like those aeroplanes that everyone admires but turn out not to be commercial. More generally my friends, who were of the type my instincts made me seize on, were the reverse of Bill. They were those I looked to for approval and support, whose authority I acknowledged. It seems I needed the security of their endorsement. The third kind, like the first, was rare. It was the one in which equality seems possible or actual, and condescension has no operative scope.

Bill was my companion through the icy heights and densities of January and February, 1947. In Wellington boots and coats and hats we made our way among the buried canes weighed down with snow much thicker than their branches but which stuck to them as if glutinous – until, that is, we gave it a good shake and it collapsed in airy powder and coagulated thudding blocks. When, however, that freezing time was over and we were moving into summer we could inspect, close up as if we were biologists, the creatures on those very canes and leaves, such as the spiky caterpillar, whose progress along a stalk was like the rippling going through a set of railway carriages as, beside a platform, they are being joined up to their engine.

With Bill my fellow observer once again, but this time in the guise of musicologists, we would attend the lane's invasion by the ranks of the Salvation Army, marching up and down or stationary as they played their stirring anthems. Out of respect and awe, and most in fear of getting in their way, we stood well back, against the wall or in the garden, ceding territory to their mission. And so they marched, their gaze ahead of them or at the music on their stands, their only gestures those determined by the nature of their instrument or role, whether this required blowing into their trombones or banging on their drums or keeping tempo as conductor. And then, at an order from their leader, which was too private to be seen or heard by us, for whom it was not intended, being only for the band's attention, as suddenly as they'd arrived they would depart again, vanishing at the road beyond, with a sharp turn to the right or left, in the same way as they'd entered.

With Bill, but not without him, I would as April

came, then May, go up into the field that stretched, it might have seemed, interminably up towards its back view of the high street, except that the High Street wended further up the hill and the true and actual high street, which went across the market square, was – being lower – named as such. It would have been too daring for me to enter the field alone, and even with Bill to share the danger I was on my guard, since while I never knew who owned it I had the sense that it was owned, and by someone who might confront us as its owner in no friendly spirit but as perhaps an angry farmer, which seemed most likely, since in it during summer we could disappear among the wheat or barley. Once, though, I was taken by my mother, or it might have been by Pauline, to the very top and through a gap that opened up there to the street, along which to the right was Pauline's father's dairy. I think now of those moments going up or down the field as in effect an English real life imitation of the Monet painting[6]. But the field had not the means to stand alone for such a purpose and long ago was taken over for development. As a reminder or memorial there is a small square grassy rump that was its base and starting point – as stark a loss as if a woman's glossy hair had been sheared off, to leave behind a residue of bristle.

I had less contact with Virginia than I had with Bill. This was only natural, though there were also other

---

[6] "Wild Poppies"

reasons. She wasn't merely older but also taller than I was and would have treated me accordingly. She wore her dark brown hair in plaits and had a mild attractiveness of the sort some other people have which renders them agreeable but not, eventually, desirable. There was in my unfocused view of her what was socially an anomaly. I was conscious that her house was bigger and also at the end, detached, facing out towards the busy world that hurried past so urgently. And what was more her father was a doctor, of professional standing and in general practice. Yet my being impressed by this to the extent I seemed to be was odd, unless it came from unawareness, for my father also was a doctor, and an officer in the army – facts which may have been as yet obscure to me. Nearer at hand, however, than my father was his father, who lived in a substantial house high up above the village and was said to be prestigious and revered, a person of authority among his patients and an austerely handsome man with much appeal to women, who moreover had been a student in Vienna and might even have encountered Sigmund Freud. He was someone whom I hardly knew and whose public reputation as a man of principle was largely built, I was to find much later, on means he had for personal discretion.

There is, however, to link me with him a single photograph. Taken in his garden, it is a posed affair in which my father also features. He, in a suit and tie, is holding me, a baby not yet one, and looking towards the camera. Of this very early meeting, which may also have been a very brief one, I have no recollection and know of it only from the photograph. Meanwhile, on my other side, my father's father, also in a suit but in bow tie, stands facing inwards but also a little forwards, so that his gaze, behind his rimless spectacles, looks straight past me and past my father, and has within it a smile faint enough not to be admitted but ironic and removed.

CHAPTER IX

UNCLE GEORGE'S PUNISHMENT

Life took me away from Uncle George and from all thought or recollection of him – except when on my birthday or at Christmas I received his postal orders – until my childhood was behind me and I was sitting reading one May morning in my College garden. I had never sat in it before and I don't think ever did again. It was one of those coincidences in which time combines with place in order to deliver an unlikelihood whose nature may make us wonder at the mystery of life's management. I just happened to look up towards the bridge that crossed the river and the sun that shone above it. Two men were coming over it towards me. Did I recognise my uncle after so many years of disconnection and, it might be said, oblivion? Or did he recognise me? Perhaps he had been looking for me, knowing I was in Cambridge and that, even if I eluded him, it was in any case the sort of place to visit. We waved to each other, perhaps he first, and I joined him

123

on the bridge. His friend, Leo, a shorter man of thicker build, was introduced, and opened up at once on the 'conducive ambience'. This wasn't George's sort of talk, which was more studied and grammatical. There must have been a hesitance brought on by George's awkwardness with me and mine with him and by the fact I had become, if only just, or even not yet quite, an adult, while having a need to be perceived as one. I took them with me to a pub I used, where they joined me in some beer and pie, my daily menu. Soon afterwards we parted. I don't recall where they were staying or were going, and gradually my memory of the visit faded.

A few years passed before two incidents took place in close succession which had a link that only now occurs to me, though it may have struck at least my mother at the time, and possibly and more crucially my father. Which of them came first may have its bearing on my father's treatment of my uncle; not that my father, whose nature (and perhaps nurture) lent itself to cruelty, would have deemed his action other than medicinal. Of one of them I was the victim. It caused me deep embarrassment, and even now keeps up the trick of reappearing when my mind, off guard, imagines it is safe elsewhere. The other brought to a head my uncle's inner trauma, and would have been a major factor in his final act upon the earth, which as he was a kindly man would have distressed him.

I never once observed my father and my uncle George together and can't envisage how they would have found a mental rendezvous, unless it was in each's intimacy with my mother, though the manners of their intimacy with her naturally differed.

It was when my parents were in Paris, at Saint-Germain-en-Laye, which they had arrived at from a previous *beau monde* astride the island of Victoria, Hong Kong. My mother had invited Uncle George to stay. Did her undisguised enjoyment of her cousin's presence irritate my father? George shared with her some cultural interests such as the theatre and ballet, which my father was quite closed to and, in the blunt way that he had, disparaged. And naturally he could do so with all the standing of a doctor and a brigadier. But my mother would have much enjoyed this chance to go about with George, guiding him through the worlds of Saint-Germain and Paris.

My parents rented an apartment looking out across the valley to the woods that rose beyond it and in the heat of the Parisian summer, as the late morning turned to afternoon, shimmered and vibrated with an intensity that, natural to France, largely denies itself to England. England perhaps is all the dearer for its holding back, and France the more seductive for its emphasis.

My mother would of course have taken Uncle George to see the Chateau, both its Musée with its Bosch and its garden with its ranks of foliage. And they would have walked along the terrace looking down towards the Seine so far beneath, and then beyond across the western suburbs to a Paris that, however hard one stared, refused to show itself. And they would have ambled past the bandstand in the trees behind them which were the offshoots of the *forêt* just beyond. Then, if their minds had turned to Paris, they could have set off on the stopping train to Saint-Lazare. It might have been they would have found their way to Chopin's grave and even caught the fleeting moments of its being dressed in that day's reverential blooms; and maybe while they were standing there they would have had in mind the pianist who, in the little house in Yorkshire, had travelled with her ageing fingers through the intricacies of the polonaises.

Did then my mother's attention to her cousin irritate my father? Did George's slight elusiveness with him, which may have been a matter of his temperament, that was always slightly diffident and hidden, but perhaps also an assertion, to set against my father's military aura, of his own success in business, come over as a provocation? Did my father's later action spring from his resentment at a sense of being excluded, not only by George and Art but more importantly my mother, who was so vitally and irreplaceably his second self? It wouldn't have been much use her telling him how silly he was being and maybe – how absurdly – a bit jealous, when all the time that they were busying themselves with things that didn't interest him he had had for company the entourage of Fontainebleau's top brass.

Intermittently in the years that followed I had reason to be grateful, morally and financially, for George's aid.

This was despite the fact our lives, which once had strangely coincided, had followed separate courses. I have sometimes wondered, thinking of him, why he should have treated me so favourably when he might as easily have not. It was perhaps a mixture of his thoughtfulness and his finding little in me to offend him or, more positively, reasons – such as my interest in the arts – to be drawn towards me. He might even have been told, not by my mother, who needed always to deny what was uncomfortable or unpleasant, but by my aunt, who had resentments of her own to nourish, about my difficulties with my father, which would have rendered me in George's eyes a fellow victim.

I drove up from the south to George's funeral, where my mother and her sister joined me, having themselves set off from Harrogate, my mother having gone to stay with her. By now my mother had remarried, my father having had a fatal heart attack which had been preceded by another several years before and which, I had to feel, must be attributable, as well as to his unhealthy mode of life, to the tensions that had always gripped him. Yet, vulnerable and irascible as he was, he was my mother's rock and had been from the beginning when, defying her admirers, he had withstood them resolutely. His departure at once removed my mother's solid ground. Emotionally and practically, she found herself unfitted to be by herself. After a brief unhappy gap she seized her chance, for almost simultaneously a colleague of my father's also lost his wife. The men had worked together, my father a rank above, and the couples had been good friends. The coincidence fell neatly into place, but for a single detail – my mother's second husband's pressing need, which he had not the means of meeting, to erase the drawback of his only having been a colonel. But in choosing him my mother hadn't let this be a disadvantage, and, in a Grade 1 Norman cloister and haute couture cream dress whose lemon tint was mirrored in the icy glaze upon the stately cake prescribed by her, she married this same colonel. At once her confidence returned, and not long afterwards she realised she had his measure. Her subservience towards my father was replaced by mockery of his successor. Her priorities hardened: she acquired steel. This affected me. Her neediness between her marriages, which had brought her closer to me, ceased. My residual illusions, which during my brief tenure had been reanimated, died.

We assembled in the large Victorian church for George's valedictory parade. Here our modest numbers as, in enigmatic solidarity, we closed towards each other at the front, gave to the massive void behind the power of a final judgement.

The rendezvous, a modern hall, was on the listless sort of road whose only mitigating feature is perhaps its exit. The hall's interior, a long, wide vista of formica and steel tubing, greeted us mechanically. The funerary lunch or tea, since the time of day was indeterminate, was already waiting, left there as if by culinary spirits, on a table near the entrance. This patently was fare that lacked pretension. It was, as banquets went, plain-spoken. One might have deemed it parsimonious. It waited to be left or taken with the blandness of its automated manufacturer. The discrepancy, when one considered Uncle George's war and post-war parties, could not have been more candid. Those had been provided in a time of dire austerity, this when his affluence had never been more topical. This second incongruity was a reversal of the first, and a mystery awaiting resolution.

Seated with my mother and her sister at a table by the wall, I had a feeling, which the nearness of the wall augmented, of a sudden closeness to these women whose importance for me had declined. But I saw an opportunity and felt a readiness for confidences. How many years, I wondered, was it since I had sat like this alone with them, two of the three women I had begun my life with? My mother had been my point of reference for those early years which seemed immutable until, suddenly, they ended and my aunt took over as her local, albeit geographically distant, representative. Then, somewhat like a colony, I at last grew restive, impatient for self-governance, which came, as it so often does, with revolution. And thus at forty, after more than twenty further years, my sense of intimacy not only with my mother but her sister was conditioned by our separations and our failures with each other, perhaps as an ex-colony may go on brooding over its resentments.

Addressing a ham sandwich I noted that, but for Kay, my uncle Jack's Canadian wife, a still imposing woman, to whom I had conveyed the sort of smile such looks invite, there seemed to be no one present I could recognise, which wasn't really so surprising. Most of the people from my early childhood were already dead: all of my mother's parents' generation, naturally, and many of her own, and of the remainder yet others had been unable or unwilling to attend.

Some names coming up of cousins of my mother's who had all been designated aunts of mine or, in the usual Yorkshire parlance, "aunties", my mother fondly mentioned Auntie Win. This led me to put a question springing from the instant sharpness of a memory that even now I had to hide from them. I asked, therefore, as if not sure: hadn't she had a daughter?

'Pauline? You must remember her? A very pretty girl. You were her favourite. You were always wanting to be with her.'

'You adored her,' Shirley emphasised. 'There was nothing you liked better than her having you on her lap.' And she recalled something about her I'd forgotten: 'She always had a large bow ribbon in her hair.'

'On the right side, I remember,' said my mother.

Later, both regretted, she had coarsened: had gone to seed and lost her teeth. She had been adopted as a baby from sources that were obscure and questionable. It was as if they knew the truth about her dealings with me and wished to banish my illusions.

'I thought there would have been more people,' was my mother's next reflection.

I said it did seem rather on the thin side. There were hardly any present of my age or younger. I supposed that all those people he had known in business had by now dispersed and vanished.

'I didn't think there'd be so many, in the circumstances,' was my aunt's assessment.

My mother glanced at her. It seemed she had ventured where she shouldn't. This made me curious.

I said, 'When I last saw him, down in Cambridge, he had a friend with him I don't see here, unless the one I'm thinking of is incognito or has greatly altered.'

'Leo, you must mean – the last person I'd expect to see here,' said my aunt. 'It was all so very different in the days when they were travelling through Europe – in Spain or Italy or Greece or…'

'Cambridge,' my mother said with a bathetic smile.

'You're thinking of our meeting when I took them to the Eagle, or was it the Baron of Beef? One of them, perhaps the latter. It was, of course, long ago.'

I was in this reminding them, as a man now middle-aged and bearing duties and responsibilities both as a father and a husband, that such times were far behind me and almost indeed beyond my range of vision.

My aunt wondered who had paid the bill. If George was present it was usually him.

In this case, I assured her, I had paid it. 'It was

nothing to write home about.' It couldn't have been, given my modest allowance. 'But it was a token thank you for the years of postal orders.'

'Yes, he was very generous, but so were your other aunts and uncles,' my mother pointed out as if I risked forgetting them.

My aunt's whole mind, however, was on Leo. Leo, she informed me, was the sort of friend who couldn't simply be dispensed with when his time was over. He had the tenacity of a crab. It was, in her own knowledge, many years since George had tired of Leo's grip. But Leo was too pertinacious to be shaken off. His insensitivity was his strength. Thus he was there until poor Uncle George's end, and had much helped, she thought, to bring it on. For George's ailing heart the struggle had proved too great, and he escaped from Leo to the imagined refuge of a hospital. Yet not there either was he secure, for Leo came to plead his case, looming over him in his bed. And in spite of George's pleas to have him banished Leo was party to his final moments, which he accompanied, it had been attested, with recriminative shrieks and wailings. George could have taken little pleasure in this last encounter with humanity. The incident, which had not reflected well on the administration, had led, however, to some changes in the regulations and procedures.

She knew all this at second hand, from gossip in the family. It had been a sad end for him. He had been a decent sort of man, though a victim of his weaknesses,

132

which had proved his tragedy.

I heard my mother sigh – something she did when she was wishing to discourage what was being said and what, she might fear, was still to come. She was, however, at the mercy of her younger sister, who had the bit of George's case between her teeth and had also given rein to curiosity in me. Already I was calling up my memories of that unexpected day in Cambridge.

I asked, to make sure of what I'd sensed, what had been Leo's "issue". My aunt's glance showed surprise. Perhaps she was forgetting my great distance from my family, both in place and time and, it had to be acknowledged, in emotional connection. But she then proceeded. Given all those years that they had lived together, Leo had, she said, arrived at an assumption of his moral rights: that should he survive George he must be in pole position. He would have set his mind on this, especially as, with Leo's full connivance, George had been growing isolated from his family, by whose negative reception of his friendship he had been affronted. And in Leo's mind his case was boosted by his lack of other means or assets, his having given up, to serve George as companion and indeed factotum, employment that had been not only gainful but fulfilling, which was a claim much challenged, although with little inside knowledge, by all the family parties with an eye on George's fortune.

'It would explain his absence,' I proposed, 'if George had finally disappointed him – if he had almost grasped his dream like Gatsby?'

'It would,' replied my aunt, whose eyes, behind her glasses, seemed to encompass more than Leo though not Gatsby.

'I feel a kind of sympathy,' I said, 'if they were all that time together. He would have had his expectations.' For now I'd turned my mind to Dickens and a favourite novel (in which I could revisit, but sitting in my armchair comfortably away from them, my own discomforts and embarrassments).

I noted that my mother was still silent.

'Sympathy wasn't something that he much attracted,' my aunt informed me in the dry tone life had brought to bear in her. 'He took George from his family in a way that was resented. And George was well aware of this, and also of the withdrawal of support. As time went by George saw, I think, what others did: that he was bogus and pretentious, but which for so long he had either failed to see or not allowed to trouble him because...'

She paused, judiciously.

'Of loneliness, perhaps?' I said.

'Well, he was lonely, certainly.' This was a mere concession to an answer she could have given, and almost had, but for her prudery.

The effect was George's growing separation from his roots. That people didn't take to Leo or to his place in George's life became more difficult for George as he began to spot the causes of their animosity, revealed more by their distance than their presence. No one, she imagined, would have gone so far as to be frank with him (as she, a moment earlier, had failed to be with me).

'English people have,' I said, to press the matter, 'a genius for tacit condemnation.'

She let this pass without remark, but then, having gone so far already, gave way to a desire to be more open. It seemed to be the case, she told me, that although he was always on the surface his old self and had at last become quite painfully aware of what had long been obvious to his relations, the nature of his lover, the unhappiness that they had caused him in the meanwhile, when he might still have been enjoying his illusions, festered. Thus she admitted George's circumstances, which, although by now I felt I knew them, I had heard her unambiguously state.

I took it as implicit that Leo had come adrift with George financially. It seemed now very likely that his nieces and his nephew, the children of his two brothers, would be beneficiaries, and that first cousins like my mother and my aunt would not have been entirely overlooked. I mentioned just the nieces and the nephew.

It seemed they had been omitted. My mind turned instantly to my mother, with whom he had shared a strong affection as well as a devotion to the theatre, musicals and ballet. I sensed, however that with Shirley he had less in common, partly because she had always been the younger sister in the background and also, unlike my mother, introverted – lacking confidence;

besides which she had always seemed uninterested in the arts. Hadn't the bitterest of our arguments concerned a painting – I think by Monet – I admired which, in an opposing spirit, perhaps because I was too positive, she found no merit in? Despite this I should have liked my aunt, who had never been well off, to have had reason to be grateful to my uncle. But my main ambition was for my mother. I was mindful also of contenders such as Kay, who while unrelated to him had been married to his brother, whereas a cousin, even a first one, was more distant than a sibling; indeed her manner, when I glanced at her, was that of a person well at ease with life. But I could remind myself I had no memory of her ever looking otherwise in spite of what had surely been a not entirely satisfactory marriage.

Since they were still denying me the answer I was nervous of, I was obliged to put my question, which I came at sideways. From this I learned they too had not been mentioned but were putting down their failure very bravely to his oddness. My mother couldn't help revealing, when I wondered if she wasn't even so a little disappointed, that she had hoped that he would leave her Auntie Ada's emerald brooch, which she had always coveted, a fact George had in his possession, it had seemed to her advantage, though in that she was to find herself deluded.

'That was before he came to visit you in Paris,' said Shirley meaningly.

'He had a really lovely time with us,' my mother

136

countered with some heat.

My aunt remained, however, undeterred, peering upwards through her glasses in denial.

My mother now appealed to me: 'I took him everywhere. We went inside the Chateau and around the gardens, and all the way along the terrace. He absolutely loved the view across the river into Paris, although even for someone with good eyesight it's hard to pick out much beyond Le Vésinet.' (It must have been anxiety to justify herself that made her speak so carelessly in front of Shirley). 'But it was the rue au Pain and the patisserie, where he bought some gateaux and some chocolates as a present for me, that were for him the *tour de force*.'

'A busman's holiday,' my aunt rejoined.

'And I took him on the train to Paris, to the Louvre, where we had some lunch, and then to Notre Dame.'

'You didn't get to Père Lachaise?' I said, at once suspecting that they hadn't and fearing he had missed it.

This puzzled her. It was beyond her compass. I said that Chopin's grave was there and every day his lovers came and put their flowers on it. I had watched an Asian girl, just coming into bloom herself, intently laying out her posies and bouquets… It was a place, I said, to bring back memories of Edith. At this my mother's eyes grew watery.

Shirley suggested I should help her get some cake, supposing no one wanted jelly, which for a funeral was, she thought, a very curious sort of choice and couldn't surely, as she knew he had disliked it, have been George's. There was also tea or, she imagined, I'd prefer the coffee. Leaving my mother to her memories, which I could see were melancholy, my aunt and I departed from the table.

'You ought to know,' she said, 'that she is doing what she always does, faced with a reality that proves too much for her. She is making up a past from which the bits she doesn't care for disappear.'

Of course, this made me eager to hear more. Conveniently, I saw that Marion, another of George's cousins by his father's brother, had stopped beside our table and was talking to my mother, who had stood to greet her. It was the leeway that I wanted.

Apparently on his final evening George had been my father's guest for dinner at a restaurant, my mother having gone down with a sudden unexpected virus and retired to bed. It meant, of course, my aunt said, that my father had my uncle to himself. It seems he had told my mother that he felt it his professional duty to say something to him, and it would be better done outside consulting rooms. Indeed, the restaurant was no antiseptic surgery but among the most prestigious gastronomic venues France could offer. It was in fact that very one withdrawn a little in its exclusivity from the meeting of the Chateau gardens with the public terrace, and overseeing, from its hidden vantage points, the Seine: it was the celebrated Pavillon of Henri IV. Here my father had contrived to trap my uncle in a

138

setting perfectly designed to overwhelm him with a sense of obligation, even gratitude. The dinner was arriving at its end when, having waited till that final moment, my father set about his actual purpose, which was, as a doctor and a Christian, to address the other's abnormality. At which George stood up from the table. My father answered this with eyebrows raised. George said he wished to pay the bill. My father said it was already settled.

It had been, George had reported back in Yorkshire, the most unpleasant ending to a dinner he had ever been subjected to. He had been my father's physical and moral prisoner. For he had given George to understand, in the ungentle terms at his disposal, that his condition, for which he could refer him to a specialist in London, was a matter not merely criminal but pathological. He was, bluntly, diseased. There were, however, drugs available to help him. My father, his junior in age, had addressed him with the punitive demeanour of one familiar with the appertaining law and fully consonant with its morality.

I too had been found to be diseased, but in a more general manner: with inadequacy. And as I thought this, with some pity for myself, my father reappeared before me, above the jelly and the currant cake. My eyes while he was taking stock of me were forced towards his clipped moustache, which as he began to find me wanting coalesced in disapproval with his upper lip, itself so thin as also to assume the character of being clipped.

My father's homily to George, which perhaps, out of consideration for his dignity or perhaps security, my uncle would have watered down, acute distress had made him share with others; and the sympathy of some was fuelled by their own complaints and grievances against my father. It was my aunt, she told me, who had given my mother all the details, which she had repelled indignantly. For my father kept such matters from my mother as not fit subjects for her ears, which were too delicate, perhaps too womanly, to receive them. And it seemed that George also on his departure the next morning had spared my mother any troubling insight into his experience. But Shirley had been robust about it: my mother had needed to be told what George had said. She had been always too protected from realities of an upsetting sort, which ostensibly she was too sensitive to handle. In fact, my aunt confided as we turned our backs upon the buffet, my mother was made of a complacent metal no threat to it could get through.

I had reached the point in my experience of her that made this wholly plausible. It struck me from what she did, particularly since her second marriage, that her sympathies, in which, growing up, I had had so much to trust, marched meekly to the sluggish tune of her convenience. If, though, she had been as ignorant of my father's intervention as she claimed, wouldn't she, the moment she was undeceived by Shirley – since she would have believed her partly even in refusing to –

have needed to approach my father with the simple question: was it true? My aunt had also made it known to her that all the family had been informed by George about his mortifying stay in Paris, and this particularly distressed my mother, who insisted she had "pulled out all the stops" to make George feel at home.

She would have put the question anxiously, my father being the person she most lived for, wished to please, and the rough ground of whose temper she had had much practice in negotiating. She would have been worried on two fronts: not only about her own relationship with George, which – not that she'd done anything to upset it, quite the contrary – was, it appeared, at risk, but also about her general standing in the family, which from such a distance and after so many years of separation she was not well placed to oversee. She would have needed to be reassured that whatever he might have said with every good intention although with not the greatest tact perhaps had been intensified by George's sensitivity, for as an artistic sort of person he was given to feeling and reacting disproportionately.

My father would have been exasperated: with George, with Shirley, with my mother. It might have come as a surprise to him that George had publicised a matter quite so sensitive. He would have thought that to have followed his advice, which he had not been sure he would do and had rather thought, from the rigidity that had confronted him, he wouldn't, and now was

141

certain that he hadn't, would have been to go as far as would be politic in owning to his sickness. That he had now in some way or another broadcast his disorder showed how unaware of it he was. As for Shirley's indiscretion, which she would, he feared, have taken pleasure in committing, it was a symptom of her grudges that the years had kept accumulating. He and she had never seen eye to eye and never would, although their forced link through my mother had obliged him to be wary of her, in so far as he considered her at all.

My mother troubled him because she knew about this delicate matter and that he had kept it from her, which from various angles could be seen by her as a disloyalty. George was her first cousin and one she had always got on well with, although this was now perhaps in question. My father would have had recourse to his impatience. He had merely as a doctor given George some medical advice that was intended for no other purpose than his benefit. Frankly, he was concerned about him not merely medically but legally. To have gone about the highways and the byways of West Yorkshire advertising his condition had been by any standard ill advised. And he would have told her in conclusion that he washed his hands of it. His advice had not been wanted. By way of answer he could only say that it had cost George nothing. It had been offered gratis.

At this point also my mother would have dropped the matter but with a sense of great unease at the associated guilt which doubtless the entire family now attached to her. It didn't help either that she almost never saw them, so that the popularity which from being a little girl she had been able always to rely on might have been draining from her. Yorkshire had become to her almost a foreign country compared with, for example, Egypt or Hong Kong, from which these days most of her friends derived. She feared her family was unlikely to provide her with an opportunity, not to justify my father's action, since it would have been something that she much regretted, but to explain my father's nature, which was not well understood. While he was very well intentioned and in fact soft-hearted, he lacked the verbal and emotional means to show this. He meant so well and yet came over differently. Some of them, she liked to hope, would feel sorry for her as his wife (which didn't at all mean that she wasn't happy in her marriage), and there were several she could name straight off who'd never hidden their dislike of him. She did wish Shirley hadn't told her. It would have spared her these anxieties. She had always been so well regarded, and now she had to fear she wasn't by those very people she'd grown up with and of whom she was so fond and moreover was a relation. Of course, Shirley would have told her out of spite against my father and perhaps affected by a certain envy of the very different life and situation she enjoyed and had done all these years, although with difficulties Shirley was unable, from her inexperience of them, to relate to.

I learned, whether before or after George's death I

143

am uncertain, but in any case years after my mother had left Yorkshire, of a return visit she had made with Shirley to our village and the light this shed upon the contrasts in their lives and natures. My aunt's envy of my mother was a thing whose reasons my mother knew and understood and took some strength from; for they were personal, social and financial. They had walked together through the market square which was shaped more like a triangle, with a wide top from east to west and two other sides declining at a shallow angle from it to a meeting at the bottom. It seems there was considerable disparity in recognition, all sorts of people coming up to greet my mother while ignoring Shirley, not knowing or ignoring who she was. This couldn't but be gratifying for my mother and humiliating for my aunt, who had never left the area and in fact had shown her face about the village two or three times while my mother was elsewhere, whether abroad or in the south. Besides, my mother had been always more attractive both to men and women, she was the more communicative and confident, she was certainly the more travelled, Shirley having stayed entirely and inevitably at home. My mother had had an interesting life which she could talk about quite easily, having mixed with Governors and Emirs and Lieutenant-Generals as well as the Kaid in Sudan. She had known people overseas who ran the world and also ran society as only the British – or a type of them – knew how to, whether it were officially or under cover. Once, when I

144

was visiting my family, then in Oxfordshire, I was the observer of a postscript to an evident conquest of my mother's when there was a visit to her by a secret agent – I would think from MI6 – who arrived as lunchtime was approaching with bouquets of pink and yellow roses and cream lilies. That the motive of his visit had specifically in view my mother was apparent. When, knowing professionally the value of discretion, he had gone again mid-afternoon, my mother made great light of it and said that he was lonely as such people often were and that they had known him in, I think, Khartoum. When my father came home later she reported on this visit in a spirit of compassionate amusement. That my mother had acquired admirers in my father's various postings was a thing to be more gratified than perturbed by as attesting to her wide appeal. It must also be acknowledged that she had much skill in being flattered and in general chatter.

This life of my mother's was entirely closed to Shirley, who would have been unhappy in it and so perhaps, it might be thought on balance, was lucky to have led the pinched existence that she had in one of the more ordinary streets of Harrogate. My mother had always had a glamour – a look about her – an expectation – that her sister lacked. And this tended to make my mother rather too reliant on all things needing to be well intentioned and harmonious and too disposed to shut out anything that was contrary. Shirley, who had always been denied the easiness my mother had, was the more able to see people for what they were and even, because she was controlled by it, took strength from others' negativity. My mother had had her rosy view of George's visit dashed and had resisted seeing this, whereas Shirley, who had never been to Paris or even northern France, was able to enjoy a certain *Schadenfreude*.

Humiliation touched me too in Saint-Germain, and at its centre also was a restaurant, although a different one which was, I think, in Marly. Whether my own case followed George's or preceded it is something I shall never now discover. But the time between them must have been two years at most, since my parents had arrived in France late on in 1962 and left it three years later, and the incident I am coming to took place in either 1963 or 1964 – in the particular context almost certainly the latter. If I preceded George in my ordeal, which, though it was a secret I had bound her to, my mother might have found herself unable not to pass on to my father, knowledge of my own case might have sharpened up his tone with George. If, however, it had followed George's visit, whatever measures were then taken or avoided by my father in the upper echelons of Fontainebleau is also something I shall never know, for in general my parents' lives and thinking ran on separate lines from mine and weren't regarded as my business. If I was told things, usually by my mother, I had to see this as a favour.

It was my father who was the instigator of my

embarras. He was concerned about my future and my aptitude for such professions as he trusted. It was already a misfortune that my interests and abilities excluded science. My interest in the arts and literature in particular was not only of no comfort to him but a source of great anxiety. He needed me to be a credit to him and seemed unable to discern much likelihood I might be. It wasn't merely that I was studying a subject, English, which would take me nowhere that would reassure him, but that my absorption in it showed me to be not, in his terms, serious.

It would have been because of this he mentioned the concern he had about me to a colleague, an accountant very senior in the European coterie they belonged to. He would have told him I had spent two years in Africa disseminating to my pupils texts which so far as they were culturally transmissible were in his opinion pernicious, being the agents of my own infections and debilities (though I taught only what had been prescribed by Cambridge boards). Perhaps he would have had in mind the author of *The Prelude*? He was a writer I had mentioned to my father some years earlier, in one of my abortive efforts to appease him, at a moment between my past and future, when this text was mentally my companion as I wandered, during summer afternoons and sometimes mornings, through the sunny lanes and villages of Oxfordshire. It wasn't only on my mind but, more vitally, on the syllabus. My reference to it only demonstrated my naivety in imagining that by such means as this my father might be pacified, for he dismissed this author, of whom patently he had heard, with the categorical information that had he been living in our own times "they would have put him in a mental institution". Such was his judgement. He saw no need to give a reason, nor did I ask for one.

He would have let this colleague know how very grateful he would be if he would "pick my brains" and disinter whatever I was thinking, specifically about my future and career, about which he had good reason to feel anxious, finding in me, he was likely to have admitted, little to the purpose. He would be grateful equally for his friend's proposal that he take me out to dinner in a little restaurant in Marly where the intimacy of the surroundings might promote that spirit of disclosure he was hoping for. Then he would tell me that this man, whose name I have not withheld but long forgotten and am choosing to call X, was likely to be interested, from a European angle, in my thoughts about Nigeria, which would have been a means of gaining insight into my capacities for analytic thinking and the bias of my *Anschauung*, if at all discernible. No doubt, to put me off the scent, he would have wanted him to seem more taken up with general attitudes and dispositions than what more narrowly I meant to do about my future. In any case the first would tend to indicate whatever scope there might be for the second. Who better than a very senior accountant, whose desk was at the very heart of European military planning, to cast his mind across my pluses and my minuses and come up frankly with the balance?

And so the evening came when X arrived in a taxi and took me off to Marly, where perhaps he lived, and to a small and modish restaurant where we sat at a small table opposite each other, with a window to the pavement that revealed the cut off lower halves of people going by within a foot or two, including young Parisian women in the sort of skirts which, later that year in Oxford, at the junction of Great Clarendon and Walton streets, would bring me to a sudden halt much like a motorist in an emergency. In showing me my wants, such apparitions wounded my composure.

Of our conversation at that cosy table my memory now is vague. I have, however, little doubt I would have made an effort to impress him with my mental subtlety while worrying about the likely bill my dinner would be costing him. I felt a deep compulsion to be "worthy of my hire" – to give him good value for his time and money. Would he have guessed my state of mind? As a favour to my father, he had arrived that evening at our door a total stranger to me. Perhaps he soon perceived my need to give a good impression of myself to someone of his standing, which is a frailty in me I have always wished I lacked, as it exposes me to condescension.

It turned out to be a question of contending with an unambiguous arrogation as we neared our journey's end, having at my disposal only that kind of English compromise which, showing no evidence of its seam, marries deterrence with politeness. How many inarticulate metres in the dark void of that taxi came between me and deliverance? But at last it pulled up, ticking over, and I fled.

I was, arguably, unscathed. The gentleman had, however, imposed his sensibilities on my good manners. It seemed to me at once a most foolhardy risk he had engaged in. His personal circumstances were unknown to me, I being the focus of inquiry and he my auditor. He had as well the benefit of his age – he was, I imagine, in his fifties – and also the authority of his position, whereas I was thirty years or so his junior and might have led him (something perhaps anticipated in my father's briefing) to assume my inexperience. But my experience, which I suppose was average, was a part of me I guarded from the world. I conveyed, I think, a greater inexperience than I possessed.

I was choosing, going up in the lift, between the possibilities: that either he was well practised in amours begun in restaurants and pursued in taxis or that, unhappy in his domestic life, he was searching for some sort of tender friendship of the Grecian kind. Without my knowing it, I might have offered him a signal he'd misapprehended, but, whether or not I had, he had placed himself in danger. How well did he know my father? He would have known he was inimical to "Art", and a smiling reference at the dinner table to this foible, intended I suppose by X to reassure me of his own more sympathetic view of it, was evidence. Yet could he not, an analyst at least of figures, have seen into my father's homophobia, which was not well hidden? It was surely not a thing a man in his position would have treated lightly. He was, though, fortunate in my awareness of his insecurity and of the need he had of my discretion. I didn't wish him harmed by his incaution or presumption. On the other hand, I felt affronted by his trespass.

My father was not at home, which made it all the easier to share my burden with my mother. I felt unable to contain it as a secret. The condition, however, of my speaking to my mother was that she must promise not to tell my father. She realised at once that I was serious and that she must respect this. I stood some distance from her in her bedroom as, propped up on her pillows, she heard me out in silence and with a look I saw as reassuring. I could believe she was concerned for me, knowing that I was troubled. I had always sought, in spite of some discouragements, to think the trust I placed in her, whatever else might prove delusive, was something I could rely on.

She promised to say nothing to my father. Was she alarmed or horrified by what I told her, or was it something she would rather not have known and have had to bear the knowledge of? I took her reticence to be sympathy in which there must be also shock, and there was about her face a stare implying that. I also took it that the promise she had seemed to give me would be kept. I further knew, however, from many years before, when I had been a child, the order of her priorities and loyalties, and so I realised such promises could not be absolute.

Though I never heard about it from my father, this didn't mean my mother hadn't spoken to him. If she had done, what might have been the reasons for his silence? There is of course the general problem of his failure to communicate, it seemed, with me particularly, and I had the constant feeling that it came most readily to him to find me wanting. I saw myself as placed outside the world that gave him satisfaction, as someone fated always to fall short of his requirements.

He might have seen fit to treat the incident as insignificant, in the larger picture of no account. What harm had I really come to? Hadn't it occurred, he had gathered from my mother, in the last few moments of our journey back to Saint-Germain, when there would have been no time for any actual damage to be done? X could have been intending nothing serious. It was more a gesture than an action, perhaps certainly an inept token of his good wishes for my future, in which I had admitted he had seemed to show a sympathetic interest?

He might, and this seems plausible, have felt the weight of his responsibility (pursued however in all ignorance of X's "case", for he must now see it as a case much as my uncle was a "case") for placing me in such embarrassment; which being so, he might have thought he owed me an apology, though in all our painful contacts I don't recall I ever had one from him.

He might, since guilt was something he had come to link with me, suspect that I had given by my very manner an impression of accessibility, which apparently had been deceiving. And he would yet again regret the gap between his wishes as a father and whatever it was he made of me.

And somewhere among these possible reactions was the motive for inaction, if inaction seemed to him the prudent and judicious course, for which X would show his gratitude implicitly while searching for some insight into what if anything I'd told him (I could at least presume they'd had some sort of dialogue about my readiness for my future).

My mother, however, may have spared him all this anguish by protecting him from knowledge and both of them from the uncertain outcome of his taking up the matter in the very seat of Allied Powers. She may, of course, have failed to keep my secret and he, unknown to me, have deemed it was his duty to look into what was only an unproven and no doubt mistaken allegation. His action in the case of Uncle George showed that, like Mrs Norris in Jane Austen's novel[7], he had a "spirit of activity".

Returning to our table, I resumed the subject of the will and the identity of beneficiaries. My mother and my aunt exchanged a look that now was one of mutual

---

[7] *Mansfield Park*

understanding and, had it been between two doyennes of the theatre, would have been signalling the moment of the plot's reversal. They could take comfort, and I saw they did, in the totality of the disappointment. The will amounted to an absolute rejection of us all, of which this present occasion, which he had arranged so very sparingly and in denial of his generous nature, was a lucid symptom. For no one at all had been remembered, not even with a brooch. The disaster was in common. No one could resent another's preference, in which context all who had still a mind to it had turned up to this lunch for which he had set aside the very moderate provision we had economically consumed. And now my mother and her sister were united once again in analysing George's vengeance on "the whole pack" of his relations, many of whom, including me, he had always generously aided.

He had felt misunderstood – mistreated – victimised. Leo had made him alien to his family. He was still, though long retired, a very wealthy man, and had had the benefit of sound advisors. The identity of his heir was a reproof not instantly perhaps quite comprehended. His whole estate, I gathered, had been gifted to a building company which specialised in low-cost housing linked to a charitable mission statement. I shared my mother's and her sister's consternation at this outcome. It didn't strike me till much later that the beneficiary and I had much in common, since some years earlier, just after I became a husband, George's loan, which was entirely free of interest, had made it possible for me to buy a property, a little Kentish cottage. There was in George a wider kindness and humanity which his retributory will presumably enacted. Perhaps he had borne in mind my mother's father's ruin in the 1930s and my family's sad departure from their much loved home.

CHAPTER X

ADULT CRIMES

I had much to do at the beginning with my mother's wider family, which was intimately spread about the village and in the towns and other villages surrounding it. In those days such convergence was the norm, and relations might provide the bulk of those one saw as friends. When aged five I left the village with my mother and my little sister I also left that life behind. The village and its people grew as distant almost and as separate from me as the world I was about to enter. My perspective altered with my geography. Changes of location switch my feelings' sense of gravity. To that extent they are adaptable. Yet certain key emotions reach beyond the boundaries of time and place, reminding me of what is lost, most probably in many instances for ever. It is a mortal recognition age accentuates.

Not even, however, at the beginning was I at all connected with my father's family, just as I wasn't with my father. I had at the time some very faint and crude perceptions of my father's parents and later not much clearer ones. I was like a person filling in a jigsaw for which nearly every piece is missing. Thus my father had an elder brother who, though as a child I never came across him, had over him in my imaginings the shadow of his notoriety. He was, it seemed, a person it was almost criminal to think of let alone to mention.

My father's father, whose respectability has been acknowledged, kept up a separate establishment in a city near enough for his convenience but far enough, in days when motor-cars were not so common, for that obscurity so necessary to him in the conduct of his business and profession. Here lived his mistress with her sons, whose paternity I never learned and about which I can only guess.

In spite of his precautions, natural to such men of wealth and standing, my grandfather was, it strikes me, cavalier in his employment of discretion. At least, my father when he became a student was confronted with the truth. It seems that, when it was a matter of my father's studying medicine, he had only a single option in his choice of university. He must attend the one located in the city of his father's other residence. This served the purposes of thrift as well as academic reputation, since the particular institution was well thought of and, among the universities, could hold its own. There was no need for the expense of living at a distance and incurring the associated costs of board and travel. But his niggardly allowance made even paying for his lunches difficult. To this his father had an answer ready: he could take them at his mistress's, who would provide them for him.

My father, however, spurned this chance of intimacy with his father's lover. Perhaps his father hoped he might in time grasp better what it was he saw in her and thus acquire more sympathy for his position. Perhaps it was to test or to develop his maturity, whether sexual or moral. Perhaps his son would be obliged to see, or even to admit, the gap in quality between his mistress and his wife, my father's mother, and so give credit to his aesthetic judgement which, if it had had to be determined on the basis of his mother, would have been harder to substantiate. Perhaps there was no part of this of any interest to his father. Perhaps he only wished to show him who was master. Yet need and determination served my father well. His skills in bridge and poker subsidised his freedom.

So much of my father's past remains a blank spot in my mind. I was never party to his confidences. If he did confide in other people, he must have found in them an understanding that I lacked, since in my middle thirties I was still unready to be trusted by him, even as an executor, a stance that had bewildered his solicitor, who informed me later that only with some difficulty had he persuaded him not only of my suitability but my actual capacity. That I already held the rank of a Vice-Principal, though of a minor institution, was for my father clearly immaterial.

Among the reasons for my lack of contact with my father's family was his own absence, not merely until the war had ended but for the two years afterwards in London, to which he had been posted and where, at the War Office, his military ambitions were beginning to consume him. No longer was he a territorial but a committed regular. His life had been given to the army. General practice had been foregone. His father had been repudiated. And now there could be no question of a return to Yorkshire.

My father's mother, by the time that I appeared, was a very sickly invalid arranged, was my impression at the bed's foot, to gaze across her bed clothes from the mountain of her pillows with an expression that was unintelligible. I have only that brief memory, when I was taken by my mother up the hill above the market square to a house perhaps larger and older than any other I had ever been in. Withdrawn among its trees and shrubberies and lawns with open land and fields beyond, it had a view across them of the upper reaches of a Georgian or post-Georgian building with a pediment. It would have been a nonconformist church or chapel – afterwards, having served its time, demolished. It was either from that first visit or a later one that I recall the climb up each deep step on to a landing of great length along which stood a gleaming line of panelled doors shut fast against the world's approach. Between these doors, interred within gilt frames, were sombre visages whose eyes responded to my timid interest with an impassivity that was unblinking. These likenesses of beings I could never come to know nor even to identify were those of my progenitors from whichever side, paternal or maternal, of my father's heritage they came to be there. We made, however, the crossing of that passage in which only the hall clock down below, by virtue of its own long standing and antiquity, had licence to be heard. And at the further end my mother knocked and was admitted by a faint reply that came out either through the door or round its edges. Inside, my mother took the chair provided for her close beside the invalid. From my own removed position at the bed's end I was able to look upwards through the bars across the heavy folds and rolls of quilt between us at a very round-faced woman with glasses also circular, their frames bright black in keeping with her hair which, parting in a geometric manner at its centre, adhered on each side to the contours of her skull. I also noted, having leisure for this, that in the very middle of her leaden cheeks a rash of purple veins made up a cross-stitch. From time to time this woman I had never seen before, who was my father's mother, stared impenetrably through my being. If at any point she spoke to me I have no memory of it even now as I am looking at her from the bed's end trying to remember. But I imagine I was supernumerary.

This may have been the only time I ever saw her, and her stare may have comprised not only her evaluation but farewell, since between that visit and our life abroad and our return in 1949 she was already gone, though the time and manner of her going were for me no less opaque than all her life before that.

*

I mentioned earlier my father's father's mistress and some sons she had, whose paternity or paternities lay wholly outside my knowledge, which concerning all this second family of my grandfather's was sparse. What follows, therefore, is a mixture of the actual and possible, drawing on my conjectures and hypotheses.

His mistress was Australian and a nurse. They met each other in the First World War, at which point he was entering his forties and would have been established as a doctor. After the war, from some point undetermined, he kept her in a city house he had some miles from where he lived and practised. Either after his wife's death or his own she took possession of his own house as its mistress and lived there with her sons, whose ages are unclear, although they must have been of working age because their failure to show interest in employment was apparently a village scandal, being proof for all that they were living off the doctor's money. His death enhanced their easy circumstances, since he had left his whole estate inclusive of its chattels to the woman who had been his mistress for three decades and straight afterwards, on his first wife's death, his wife. The space in which he acted was a narrow one.

These facts link up ironically with a deceiving moment when my father seemed to warm to me. I had been sitting with him in his father's garden a day or two before the latter's death. My father had shown me something presently his father's that would pass to him and afterwards one day, he said, be mine. This was a gold watch, either a hunter or half-hunter, but which I am uncertain as it was the only time I saw it and perhaps the final time my father did. It had been the agent of our short, illusory rapprochement. And, as its disappearance showed, my father's reconciliation with his father had been merely nominal, a delusion. Perhaps his father's heart's intransigence had never faltered till at last it failed entirely.

There is another piece of evidence about his father that I have: a second photograph which shows him standing in impeccable white uniform, his elbows out, his hands into his sides, his whole demeanour one of jaunty ease, and framed becomingly by palm fronds, on a recuperative post-war voyage somewhere in the West Indies or the Balearics. His features, over twenty years before the other dating from his middle sixties, share with it the cryptic smile that that has. This one's irony conveys perhaps his self-awareness and a desire to make clear his own amusement at the spectacle he is conscious he is making of himself. And it suggests no less his vanity.

Where, in that region straddling France and Belgium,

might he have come across his mistress? In Philip Gosse's *Memoirs of a Camp-Follower*[8] there is reference to a meeting point for doctors out of Scotland, but largely out of Glasgow, with their opposite numbers from Australia and Canada. This rendezvous was in the district of Armentières, on the Franco-Belgian border. My grandfather was such a doctor out of Glasgow, and those first-lieutenants from Australia would have been augmented by the ladies of the Imperial Military Nursing Service (QAIMNS). Given the lack of facts at my disposal, that body's relaxation, early in the war, of its admissions policy is instructive: women no longer had to be unmarried or over twenty-five and furthermore were not debarred, as previously they had been, by coming from a "lower social order".

Did they meet out in the trenches or in a dressing station further back or in a hospital? Was it near the war's beginning? How old was she when he encountered her: the age of a novice or already in her thirties, not greatly younger than himself? Did he perceive at once, as in a coup de foudre, or more gradually as they worked together, that she had the very attributes his life was lacking? Did he regret already she was not the woman he had married? For he had married not a woman but a practice, having been yet another clever Scotsman desperate for a solid English future. He had defied his sexuality in gaining this. Supposing he

---

[8] P. Gosse, *Memoirs of a Camp-Follower*, Longmans, Green & Co. (1934)

regretted life's delay in bringing them together, was he given to bemoaning time's misplacement, or was he, being as he was so well established in his Yorkshire practice, already working out his future strategies and dispositions?

He was successful and good-looking and was aware of both. And yet he had not, not as yet, received from life what assets such as his would usually offer. He had not had love – not in his marriage. Within that he had not been able to explore his feelings or his senses. And so, whatever the Australian woman's age, he must have seen her as the cure for all these ills. She must have had enough in her to captivate a man approaching what he thinks of as already middle age and in a situation giving little hope of future joy or even satisfaction. He seizes his last chance, as it appears, of happiness. He sees how he can have his practice *and* his earthly bliss.

And why would she have wanted him? Speculation would be easier if I had ever known her circumstances. If she were married with three sons and had begun to feel her age almost before her time, or equally if she were very young and confident and had that kind of curious open gaze such women often have, wouldn't she in either case be drawn towards a man established and assured whose good looks were arriving at maturity and who displayed besides a readiness for devotion? Perhaps, supposing she were married, it was to a disappointing husband? Perhaps the thought of England drew her? Perhaps she had an English background, even an English past?

Somewhere among what's possible is truth. But, where there are so many possibilities which lie always beyond one's grasp, it may be as if one undertook a journey in which the choice of destination were no more than theoretical since all of them were out of reach. One turns oneself into a juggler endlessly throwing up balls which bounce back mockingly from the ground. The past is so often nothing better than a series of hypotheses and suppositions drawing on our memory's failures and confusions in which both actions and their agents change their natures from one moment to another, but where – if we do – we may come upon a truth quite different from the one we were attached to; and by this we may find ourselves affronted and may hardly bring ourselves to alter our false pictures and impressions that we have always known and stood by and in which has resided for all these years of our illusions our mental and emotional security.

My father's father, as noted earlier, was a man who as a doctor running a large practice needed to be respected in the interests both of his business and his dignity. He would have required, in his own mind, that his patients be in awe of him, as his superiority to the run of them, he would have felt, deserved. And his discretion in his private life had geared itself to this, though talk was always likely in that smallish town or village about his covert *nid d'amour* where he was said to keep a woman. Some would have been disturbed and some intrigued, some incredulous and some persuaded, some censorious and some approving. Yet when the time came to mount the hill and face him in his surgery there couldn't be any doubting his ascendancy. His commanding presence crushed all lack of faith. If he had a mistress wasn't that his business and he could well afford it, and his wife no one after all could call a beauty and some called her the opposite. His wife, they said, was no spring chicken and never had been. Poor man! He worked so hard and so successfully: how could one grudge him recreation? He hadn't married out of love – that much was obvious and well advertised – and now, or rather, the more informed ones pointed out, for a long time ever since a fateful meeting out in France, or was it Belgium, he had been making up for what he had been missing.

A question to which I have no answer is that concerning the paternity of his mistress's three sons. They might have come with her as baggage from Australia, and there's no evidence I know of that they didn't. But what established man already married with three children of his own would take on board, however smitten, the three children of another man, with all associated costs as well as their capacity to be a nuisance, and in whom there was no particle of his own invention? He would have asked himself if any woman could be worth that, knowing by then his own capacity to find another. And if, when he met her, she was childless, he had all the time he needed in the inter-war years for the increase of his progeny. Whether, in this connection, her sons resembled him or didn't I also never gathered.

There was seemingly in my grandfather a ruthlessness which could enable him to move, already in his seventies, to a second marriage when the first had barely run its course. Presumably he wanted to legitimise his mistress and her children. But to proceed also in his final will to the eradication of the sons of his first marriage might be considered brutal. Bearing in mind his need of deference and esteem (especially as he had come from Glasgow and was not a proper Yorkshireman), how could he, if only in his own interests, have let this happen? Perhaps he could because by then, already in his seventies, he had less need of patients, and also because as often happens at that late age, when one begins to weary of so much, having become more inward-looking, one's world grows smaller, more selective, less engaged with what is after all outside and doesn't matter. His friends, a different species from his patients, though many of them were additionally his patients, understood. They were like him, superior people: they were professional, business, county, some political. Among them was the owner of a Grade 1 hall which stood within its many acres out into the country. If he had needed not to stand alone such people were his reassurance. His marriage, every man and woman of them knew, had been lacking in uxorious emotion, and for reasons they could understand. They were on his side, even if for some of them with squeamish caveats. It was the more unfortunate, or as some said tragic, that his sons had, each in their own way, failed him and for that reason had been excluded from his final dispensation.

What, finally, became of his Australian consort and her sons? They were not well liked, as I have said, in Yorkshire. An old memory of being told this would suggest it wasn't long before they went back to Australia with their profits.

*

Some pages ago, in what I am now seeing as a quasi-memoir, since it is full of gaps, uncertainties and statements which may be unreliable, I spoke of my father's elder brother as a person whom my family had, for their own greater moral comfort, ostracised. I only began to learn about him when I was old enough to bear the facts, perhaps when I had reached the sixth form and was studying the English moralists and Greek tragedians. By then I should have been equipped, mentally at least, to learn my uncle's history – not that my family's judgement of my readiness would have been likely to be based on any close familiarity with my reading. He was a few years older than my father, there having intervened a sister who had died at twenty-six of cancer, having just begun her own career in medicine. I am assuming that my uncle, John, was born round 1910.

He had been, I gathered, a bright and able student in the field, a long way from my own, of engineering. I have no memory, if I ever had a knowledge, of the institution he attended. Like his brother after him he would have been acquainted with his father's mode of living. He was a boy, as I was later, growing up in time of war, his father absent and later present in a manner that was also absent. He may well have had an easy style about him drawing on his background, which was privileged; and like his father he had the sort of looks agreeable to women, which might have brought about a certain laxity, in which also his father acted as a model. He may, both as the elder and more genial of the sons, have had the more indulgent treatment, which would contribute in the end to his undoing.

One day apparently, I imagine near to 1930, a young woman, bearing upon her the signs of her condition, appeared to see the doctor in his surgery. She informed him that his own son was responsible and that he was denying it and meant to leave her in the lurch. She knew all about the courts that she could go to if she had to. She hoped she wouldn't and that he'd make his son see sense and make an honest woman of her. There was about her a rigid purpose which caused him much anxiety.

Her allegation, however, when his father put it to him, John rebutted with some scorn, in which there were aesthetic factors, since although he was much drawn to women, as he didn't mind admitting, this was not a woman he could possibly have laid a hand on even with his eyes closed. And surely his father grasped his reasoning as a man who saw what he did and may have felt some corresponding sympathy. Clearly, the girl was disadvantaged socially and educationally. She came from a low area of a nearby town. John didn't deny that he had come across her, as he had so many people, in the public houses he went into with his friends, but she wasn't someone he had ever mixed with. She wasn't among his group of people and had nothing about her that stood out. She was not, his father realised, in any way a suitable person for his elder son, although his protestations weren't per se by any means enough to clear him. That they knew each other was apparent. It was a question, however, of degree and manner. The public houses mentioned were of the sort that he himself would not have entered other than professionally. How he regretted now some of those other girls or women John had come across at university and had brought home for his approval and moreover admiration: young women who had been to Paris and knew a cubist from a hexahedron. One or two he himself had felt the draw of, to the extent of greeting them already in his heart as filial companions with whom, platonically but agreeably, he could pass away his time at dinner and muse on afterwards as chasers to his Scotch.

John swore he hadn't touched her, this girl he wouldn't even say he knew, merely that he had seen her once or twice with other people that he didn't know or hardly knew. She was, they said, notoriously promiscuous, and could have had no memory of place or time or person, being so open to all comers. Someone would have put her up to it, someone with an interest, like her father or her mother, who would seek to make the most of her predicament. Naturally they'd pick on someone who was rich and vulnerable. He meant by this, without however saying what he meant, the vulnerabilities, where women were at issue, not only of the son but more importantly the father, who depended for his reputation on his very questionable virtue. His father looked intently at him, making of his choice of language everything his son was thinking of and seeing in it crucially the danger to himself. And in the context he began to wonder if his son had failed to be sufficiently discreet, for he carried with him, in spite of all his due precautions, a fear that others knew and talked about his secret world in which he kept a mistress hidden, not so effectively however as to spare his wife the knowledge of her, though they had never met. If, as he feared, his son had found himself amid such talk, would he, as a young man who himself was much involved with women, have laughed it off or let himself be seeming to confirm it, as showing the prowess of his father? These thoughts were dangerous to John and had their bearing on his father's resolution of the matter.

He had at all costs to preserve that reputation he had so thoroughly invested in. He could not allow its demolition by his son. As to John's alleged responsibility, which could not be proved or disproved even when the child was born, there would be something he would find perverse in his association with that female. He had met and had approved the type of women he was mixing with at university. Yet sexuality, he knew this as a doctor, was anarchic: entrée to women in the upper social reaches was no sort of barrier to the lower. Other young women, perhaps encouraged by their friend's reception, in which the doctor had revealed some symptoms of uncertainty, came forward in support of her. His son, allegedly, was "known" as someone from outside who "splashed his money and what else" about their seedy streets.

That the girl had braved his surgery to begin with was, on the face of it, disturbing. It had been prudent, nonetheless, to let her see him when he could so easily have refused, not knowing what her business with him was or could be, since she was not his patient and from outside his catchment area. But the hard eyes of the unprepossessing girl – for that described her – and the harsh determination of the voice were evidence that, whatever might or mightn't be the facts (which science was as yet unable to determine), the publicity she might generate could threaten all he had achieved in Glasgow and Vienna, and at the Western Front, from which he had emerged with the M.C., which things were over and above his standing as a doctor. His reputation, though, he knew, was far from unassailable. It was all too easily assailable. Suppose he waited, with some provisional concession, if such a thing could be agreed between them, till she had had the child and took it to the family court? But how could that resolve the matter? Nothing certain could come out of it. And yet such civil proceedings might undo him. And there could be no benefit, only risk, in confiding *ante rem* in other doctors or in lawyers who, while they might well be friends of his, could only offer their opinions, not facts. Suppose he left the issue to await the magistrates, he put it to himself again. It would be some fellow he had sat at dinner with the week before concluding in his unmedical opinion that on the balance of the probabilities it was more likely that the child was John's or that it wasn't. Meanwhile the publicity would be likely to destroy him. There were Yorkshire people – journalists – who in their blunt, flat manner knew how to use their scalpels on an immigrant from Glasgow, having found him much too settled on their own patch for their liking. And so he reached his judgement. His son had proved unworthy of his trust. He had acted irresponsibly and carelessly. He could not be sure that he was not a liar. He had put him at this risk in not considering his interests (he meant the particular nature of his vulnerability). He'd assumed he'd bail him out. But he couldn't be bailed out except by marriage. On that the girl had been insistent, and so he feared had been her father and her mother (she having both, he had discovered). He had, he could have, no opinion on paternity, which was not finally the determinant. John

173

must, as the girl said, make an honest woman of her and take whatever were the consequences, although as a father he would mitigate their worst effects as far as lay within his power or his inclination.

Generally, people who saw themselves as members of the lower or the lower middle classes, who constituted in the whole region where I lived a more than comfortable majority, approved the doctor's action. He had "done the right thing" whereas his son had not. He had seen to it, however, that finally he also had. Thus in those large areas of the doctor's practice his stock went up. Among his friends, however, who were confined largely to the professional and business classes, but with a gloss put on them by what could be inserted of the upper middle or even upper classes, which was inevitably a modest tally, there were concerns and reservations. He had been too harsh on the boy, who had admittedly been foolish, even if not guilty. He had effectively wrecked his prospects – wrecked his education – wrecked his chances of professional employment – and imposed on him a dreadful marriage and a probably dreadful married life, from which soon enough he would detach himself. Like his father he would most likely take a mistress. If so, unlike his father he would not in that betray the woman who had been his benefactor but rather his oppressor. And, with any mistress, it would be a hand to mouth romance contrasting starkly with his father's well oiled ménage.

Some of his old friends became, regretfully, more distant from the doctor, who had considered his own interests in a manner that had not, to the extent he might have hoped, entirely succeeded, at the expense of his own son who, able clearly and promising, had proved, as so many young men did, incompetent and weak with women. They couldn't somehow help it. They were nature's, or their own, victims. And some thought of themselves and how they had got away with it.

My father, still at this time a schoolboy but developing some insight, was very sympathetic to his elder brother, by whom he had long been made aware of how their father had betrayed their mother; so when the time came for his own attendance at a university he was ready to convict his father not only of adultery but hypocrisy and to feel increasing distance from him.

The doctor transferred John's costs from those incurred in higher study to those of the terraced dwelling where he was henceforth to be accommodated. He was, however, to repay his father from his earnings at an engineering firm at which he had found employment; and, as it happened, John's accommodation lay between the houses of his father and his father's mistress, which would have made it all the easier for the former to look in on him as he was going by if only his front door had not been so much overseen by others' doors and windows.

From his marriage, John had three children: a girl, and then a boy and girl. It was, as people said, "as plain as day" that the first child wasn't his. In no way, all agreed, did it resemble him or either of his other children, who each looked like the other, though a boy and girl, and what was more their father. Besides, its faculties were much impaired, and it grew up not only with a hump but also a leg kept fastened in a brace, and in the blunter language of those days was diagnosed as mentally subnormal. He had been deceived and victimised. His fault, it was said, was his congenital eclecticism.

CHAPTER XI

I PLEASE MY FATHER

Although physically my father was largely absent from my life, I have reached the view he had more influence on my nature and behaviour than in fact my mother, to whom, in moments of distress, I earlier looked for the emotional protection that I sometimes got from her and sometimes didn't.

I am uncertain when or how the following occurred. It would have been somewhere within my first two years at Cambridge at a time when I was still on the goodish terms I had with Shirley. I know this because the journey that I took to see my Uncle John began from Harrogate. And so it was within the period of my also meeting Uncle George in Cambridge. There was a link between these uncles, the first my father's elder brother, the second my mother's first cousin. What linked them – these men who perhaps knew very little of each other – was the moral disapproval roused by each of them within the broader family. My uncle John lived in a kind of endless shadow through which no light of pardon ever broke, despite a general knowledge that his first child, which had brought about the scandal, wasn't actually his at all but had been foisted on him not only by its scheming mother but his no less calculating father.

As to the how, it is beyond me to determine whether, as a young adult who had begun to find his own authority, the initiative was my own or put to me by my mother, acting as my father's agent. If the former, it was a moral test case, and if the latter it was a kindly gesture I was happy to engage with. I felt pity for my uncle at his having had his life spoiled in the fundamental manner that he had, and pleasure also that he had been able finally to marry the woman he had loved so long while married to another woman he had never loved nor could have done. I wished to show my solidarity with the unfortunate but now perhaps recovered man who had not only been unjustly treated but had been reviled by those who said that he had "had it coming to him". And I wished him to perceive, whether or not I was the gesture's author, that I was calling "off my own bat". I was aware of Shirley's unenthusiasm for this visit. As a practising nonconformist she was most uneasy at the moral freedom I was showing. My act of warmth towards my uncle was, however, a statement also of autonomy.

And so by one means or another I found out where he lived, which was on the buried edges of a Yorkshire city, and arranged to go and see him, which I did by public transport whether by bus entirely or by bus and train and bus, and finally by walking through a cobbled street or maybe two or three of them resembling those I had already known in early childhood, cobbles being a standard feature of those poor environments in which my uncle John had come now to a sort of rest.

How very nice his wife was, and straightforward, and how very pleased they were to see me and to talk to me and to applaud the kind of scholarly achievements which in my uncle's case had been within his sight and taken from him before he could even taste them, like the banquet from the sinners in *The Tempest*. How very glad they were I'd made this effort to be with them, for while they didn't need my presence to be made respectable it was, as couldn't have been clearer, a fillip to their morale.

It was through my mother in Hong Kong I heard that I had also pleased and even touched my father, which had to be for me sufficient recompense, given that he communicated with me only in what he deemed a crisis, as when my mother was too ill to write a letter, or he had some piece of business to transact. I was in receipt of one such missive soon after I arrived at university. I had moved my bank account from Yorkshire down to Cambridge, which was to be for several years my base. It was a question of convenience rather than vainglory, although it may have had in it some symbolism. Learning, however, instantly of my departure from my former manager, my father ordered, no less speedily, my return. Not being yet as free and independent as I might have wished, I was as rapid in my compliance, and to this day, though I have never lived there as an adult, my bank account remains in Yorkshire at its natal branch, or rather the branch that long ago absorbed it when it became redundant.

Despite my hearing of my pleasing him, in all the years of separation of my growing up he might as well not have existed. Each Sunday morning after our return from chapel I sat with other boys at one of the long tables to compose my letter home, and in this, I expect as many others did, I put together all the "nothings to write home about" with which I skirted any mention of my actual life or feelings, not wishing to disturb my parents with such matters. In return my mother sent me letters full of her consuming social life in the Sudan and later on in Egypt. From my father, however, I never heard and soon gave up all hope of doing so. At last this led to a rebellion. Overcome by my despair, in which there was some anger, there came a Sunday morning when I sent my letter solely to my mother. Her answer was a painful one: it had hurt my father greatly that I had excluded him, which I must never do again. My appeal by inference had brought me only blame, and with it the deeper guilt I suffered from, that however much I longed to and even told myself I did, I couldn't bring myself to love my father.

Whenever I was with him, I felt like an encumbrance.

Later, when I was older and earning my own living, he would talk across the fireplace to my mother, in a voice he failed to raise above a private mutter, as if I didn't also occupy the room or on the other hand because I did. On those few occasions when he was obliged to be alone with me, as on a journey in the car, he would adopt an affable bluff manner the effect of which was less to make me grateful than uneasy and which in any case stopped short, as if a door had closed, the moment we were home again. I came to feel that, however great my efforts to placate him, I was bound to fail. My mother had a great dislike of difficulty and embarrassment and pretended none existed: if my father didn't show his feelings it wasn't because he didn't have them. Deep down, she said, his heart was warm. It was only that he couldn't let this warmth come out of him.

How far was his anger born in him, how far the product of experience? Whatever its source or sources, his fury was always primed. Perhaps his terseness linked with this. I was told once by the daughter of a friend of his in Paris, a genial Rear Admiral, that though her mother much enjoyed my parents' company she had suffered the acute embarrassment, my father having been habitually curt with her in the consulting room, of going to another doctor. And yet socially he might demonstrate what passed for levity. With peers of his or with more junior officers he commanded and their wives, he might participate agreeably enough in village cocktail parties, Church of England matins or late-night dances in the mess. Yet like me he was a child of war, cut off from knowledge of his father till old enough to be confronted with an unresponsive stranger. And more than that his father had acquired a lover and maintained a separate house with her and various sons he may or mayn't have fathered. My father, to my best knowledge, never had nor looked to have a mistress, although he might have given way to passing weaknesses. There was an unrelenting hardness in him that had served him well at university in playing bridge or poker for the sort of stakes that kept him funded. And so, when he taught me chess, another game well suited to his skills, there was no question of his giving me a knight or castle as a sop or an encouragement. He played each game to win, and so successfully that I soon lost heart for my defeats, much as he also wearied of his victories.

From my aunt Shirley I gained no comfort in the matter of my father. I have to note, however, that I doubt she greatly cared for him, to which may have contributed the shade in which he placed her husband, who, having been called up, had risen through his virtues to the rank of sergeant – not one, however, to place them on an equal footing. When I said to her, before I went to Cambridge and he to the Far East, that I had come to think I might be getting on a little better with my father, she answered with the certainty of those who look the truth, however daunting to its subject, in the face, 'You will never get on with your father,' which struck me as definitive.

I had been engaging, in pursuit of a more optimistic diagnosis, in what I am bound to think was self-delusion, since towards me, it was truer to say, his manner seemed to bear with it an anger always ready to explode.

Shirley also told me with respect to Cambridge, in what came over as a universal judgement to which she had been a party, 'None of us thought you would get in.'

My defiance of their presumptions raised my confidence a little, but I was to find still that I lacked the nerve for seizing possibilities and opportunities. My instinct was to distrust myself and all too readily assume rejection. This diffidence has harmed me. I have failed not only where I might quite possibly have succeeded with more faith but also in perceiving what I might have found within my scope. I have been too ready both to be grateful for approval and to be persuaded by rejection. Here, however, I find, I'm in good company and may take some comfort from a favourite author, Samuel Johnson, who was, as he admitted to his friend James Boswell, "more fearful of rejection than he was hopeful of success", and this at a time when his achievements were so universally saluted.

The moments that seemed to contain within themselves the insolubility of my failure with my father were ones, though I was far from knowing it, containing my eventual salvation. They were moments of emotional crisis towards which his reactions showed me yet again the depth of his indifference. And I had reason to suspect I must be disappointed also in my mother.

After the call I wept, but only partly at the rebuff, having a more urgent reason for my tears, the fear I was about to lose the woman who, suddenly, possessed me. At that turning point when nothing has been determined and minds are still unknown and unreliable, circumstance was pressing in between us.

It was as I had stood there in the central office that I glanced, on an impulse that had no seeming cause, across the aperture between the filing cabinets and beyond them to the furthest centre of my line of vision, which was the summit of the great stone staircase sweeping round there to give entry to our learned offices. On that distant pinnacle she stood as if she had only just alighted from Elysium. My eyes held me as in a vice, a fact immediately spotted by a female colleague who, in the facilitative role of intermediary, as rapidly transmitted my fixation to its source. Of this I would only hear much later, my fate long since determined.

I had become a lover to whom time had set a limit which with every moment had intensified my anguish. And then I found myself alone and desolate, fearful that not necessity but my own inertia had betrayed my heart.

I turned to my only refuge. It was nearer to midnight than eleven. The telephone, that fickle instrument, was waiting by my bed. I picked it up, grasping it as a friend, and rang the number. It was Shirley, however, who answered. I gathered that she was staying there. My parents, she declared, were not available, being at a dinner in the Mess. She wasn't sure when they'd be back but understood it might be late. However late it was, I said, I must speak to my mother. It was very urgent. I would wait up till she called. My aunt's hesitance in the face of this came over as unreadiness.

I waited for my mother's comfort to console me, for her to join me in my pain. But the time went by in silence. In despair, I rang again. Shirley informed me she had spoken to my father, who had told her they were not available. Of course, she glossed, feeling perhaps an obligation to satisfy both parties, my parents were important people and had their various social duties to attend to, and I was ringing very late. But did my mother know about it was my question to her, which she couldn't answer, since she hadn't asked him and he hadn't told her. In which case would she speak to her as soon as she was home again, however late it was by then, and say that I was waiting for her call?

No call, however, came, and at last I fell asleep. By the morning it was too late. And still, in any case, there was no word from her. I had to take my mother's failure, which I did with sorrow, as a signal of her disregard.

A few months later, staying with my parents, I accompanied them to such an evening in their Mess. I was chatting in the half-light of an alcove with an officer – who was, I think, a captain – and his wife, both of whom, it seemed, were well disposed towards my parents. Before us turned the carrousel of dancers, whose rhythms manifested their technique or else their disposition or perhaps the state of their emotions or even their inebriation. From the midst of them there suddenly emerged my father with his partner, whom I took to be the wife of a lieutenant – someone young and junior and malleable. Tall and, as he had been for many years, obese, my father made his swaying passage just in front of me, his cheek so near to hers I feared they might be touching, his pale blue eyes unfocused with a glaze across them. I watched him with embarrassment and aversion, the greater for my awareness of my two companions, but acted as if I hadn't seen him, as if he hadn't even been there, but all too certain they had seen what I had seen and were as anxious to pretend they hadn't.

Finding them sympathetic, and people I might confide in, and anxious now to show my distance from my father, I talked about our failure to communicate, my sense increasingly of a lack of common ground.

The officer's wife said freely, 'When we are young we always think our parents, being our parents, are remarkable – above the general run – superior. But the truth is that your parents are quite ordinary, with all the usual faults and weaknesses.'

I heard this as a vindication and a consolation and yet felt slighted by the gentle certitude with which this junior officer's wife felt able to inform me that, whatever illusions I might cherish, she found my parents ordinary.

CHAPTER XII

MENTORS AND QUASI-FATHERS

This chapter explores key influences on my life and outlook in the form of mentors or quasi-fathers, who acted mentally and spiritually as in effect replacement fathers. Some were my father's age or older but others my near-contemporaries and in a position rather of friendship than authority or seniority. A final sketch is of a friend who, born three months after me in Germany, has been the best of confidants who over so many years has helped to give my mind whatever balance it possesses.

Of course, I have also had my female mentors and even quasi-mothers who in my mother's absence have assumed her role. Among them the most vital of all my life's companions has been my wife of very long standing. Yet I have focused here on male mentors since it was in relation to my father that I had most need of surrogates. Though all too often distant from her geographically, I had less need to find alternates to my mother, in whom, however, my trust eventually withered. By then, however, so largely had my need of mentors.

GC

GC was a retired city banker in, I imagine, his sixties or perhaps his early seventies. He lived with his tall thin wife and two middle-aged unmarried children. The son was a London architect perhaps in his late thirties or early forties and like his mother was tall and a little gaunt, whereas the daughter was short and round. She too I gathered was employed, although I never knew in what, and seemed by her appearance to be the younger of the two.

To this whole family, not only to GC, I have reason to be grateful. They adjusted to my visits, which they had neither sought nor probably desired, with an immaculate and reticent politeness. My predictable arrivals, twice a term at weekends, had been negotiated by my father with GC. By way of preparation, a little while before my family's departure to Sudan, he had taken me to join the local Philatelic Club whose President was GC and in whose large Edwardian corner house (long since usurped by flats) the members gathered monthly. The familiarity this gave me with GC, though not as yet his wife or family, and with those areas of the house to which I was admitted, and with various local boys and girls who formed a junior nucleus, would have eased my first incursion with my bag or suitcase.

I soon perceived that GC's life at home was concentrated down a little passage leading towards a door from which some steps descended to the garden, but also just before this to another door into his study, where the ten red volumes of his British Empire stamps lined up unguarded on a shelf adjacent to a window, half the room's width and almost all its height, looking down upon the lawn below. This cramped room, when I was there, was generally occupied by members of the nucleus, who would be engaged in playing chess or lounging in the long cane chair whose soft furnishings wore all the ravages of use. From these accommodating depths they talked about their very local lives, in themselves prosaic but with appeal for those like me to whom almost the entire world was, on a daily basis, "out of bounds". They had a freedom and a home life I was very conscious of not having.

GC's preferred routine concerned his own domain and the activities, philatelic and financial, which absorbed him, though of little seeming interest to his family. In all the visits that I made there I don't recall I ever saw his wife, his son or daughter in his study. In fact I only came across them in the kitchen, where I would sit with them for breakfast, lunch and supper and listen deferentially to their arcane exchanges.

I looked forward to my visits, on which I placed a great reliance, and therefore wanted to feel sure I had

189

GC's approval and support. While this was not a certain matter, I had no reason to suspect his disapproval or that my being there was a burden to him. I never felt, however, while wishing that I could, that he had any special liking for me. He undertook what he perceived as his responsibilities, showing me always a detached consideration. It may have been because of his attendance at a school like mine he showed no curiosity about my own, which was a restraint in him I see now as perhaps indicative of understanding rather than indifference.

Being so open to the informality of his younger visitors, GC enjoyed a clientele that, through my own visits, I came to know and put some faith in. It functioned for me as an alternative society of no conceivable interest to the boys and masters at my school. I was, however, in that external context an anomaly. I saw the members of the nucleus as more established – more inward – with GC than I could hope to be and also, naturally, more familiar with each other. I was grateful that they showed no curiosity about a life which was so obviously different from their own. Outside their own experience, they left it there as one might food one doesn't recognise, or doesn't much like the look of, on the far side of one's plate. I was not a member of the nucleus but a visitor perhaps accepted as enjoying what they didn't have, some intermittent residential status at GC's.

I think now that, while over time I sensed he had an

inner core of chums, what interested GC were not so much relationships with people as activities, whether those he could conduct alone as, for example, sticking stamps into an album or working in the orchards that he owned in neighbouring roads, or those done more enjoyably or necessarily with other people, such as playing chess or setting off on car trips with "the faithful" into rural Surrey or to "Pompey"[9]. His sense of humour may have had a banker's guardedness, emerging unpredictably and taking you when you came across it by surprise, having much to do with pointing up the quirks he'd spotted in another person's nature or behaviour.

NH

NH had a double First from Cambridge. That is all I know about his background. He was the most important teacher that I ever had. He was a shortish man with hair that, combining white and grey and brown, ascended more sharply from his parting than it consented to lie flat. His eyebrows were unusually thick and went regularly up and down for unattributable reasons. His smile, which was faint and no more than a shadow, was barely intended for the public but expressive, one learned gradually to understand, of his discrimination and acuteness. Laughter was not within his repertoire.

---

[9] Portsmouth Football Club

191

He might have laughed, though I don't recall it, at some puerile inanity. His unsparing seriousness excluded humour. But of textual irony he was a master. "Practical Criticism", as it was strangely known, though not I believe by him, but essentially a Cambridge product, was the mode in which he gave me most. It was a demanding process in which short pieces from a prose work or an entire shorter poem would be put in front of one for comment and evaluation. One had to puzzle out their meanings and their quality. His brilliance as a conductor of the classroom's fumbling orchestra was not only a matter of his unobtrusive baton but of the cutting edges of the pieces he was giving us to play. It was through the entrance of NH's mind that I came across the "Metaphysicals" and their successor, Eliot:

> *Let us go then, you and I,*
> *When the evening is spread out against the sky*
> *Like a patient etherised upon a table…* [10]

NH was not a man of favourites, except perhaps discreetly, and only then respecting quality of work and mind. On the very few occasions that I spoke to him in private from below his dais I was conscious only of my awkwardness in the face of his dispassionate attention.

---

[10] T.S. Eliot, "The Love Song of J. Alfred Prufrock", *Collected Poems*, Faber & Faber

MC

MC, a Jewish boy a year my senior, was someone I only came to know when he was in his final year. As he was more an acquaintance than a friend I never knew what happened to him subsequently, but at a moment critical to my future he made a triple impact on my choices and, as it proved, development. It was he who urged me to give my thought and time to English and to seek a route through it to Cambridge. It was MC also who pressed me to read Proust not merely in translation but *ab initio* in French, and so I started on what has proved a major journey of discovery. And thirdly it was MC who, one evening half-way through our evening's preparation, brought along the corridor a book he thought might interest me. This was Berenson's *Italian Painters of the Renaissance*[11], which inspired in me a lifetime's study not only of that book's subjects but of painting of all schools and periods. It was with the greatest brevity that MC made these lasting inroads into the course my life would take, on the face of it to its advantage.

CH

CH was a polymath, as shown in the record of his publications, where OUP and HMSO vie to the former's

---

[11] B. Berenson: *The Italian Painters of the Renaissance,* Phaidon, (1952)

clear advantage. He made his debut with scholasticism and theology, going on from there to medicine and the heart in ancient Greece, German post-First World War debt, South American railways in the 1930s, and Allied governance of Italy from 1943 to 1945. His career ended with a conflation of his interests as a teacher of Humanities to Australian medical students.

I met him socially, in the later 1950s, when I was at the point of leaving school and going on to Cambridge. My parents had returned a second time from Egypt and were based in Oxfordshire, outside a village half a dozen miles from Oxford. It was a place where, if you were sociable and also socially acceptable, you might expect to hit it off with the appropriate people. My parents were soon in this position thanks to my father's military gloss. Whereas they had a high opinion of CH, they were less enthusiastic, it emerged when I was in my forties and old enough to be apprised of it, about his wife. My own view of her, however, differed very much from theirs, and she became in time a somewhat critical quasi-mother to me.

LH was, I soon discovered, Portuguese, and also, as she informed me, from the Portuguese nobility, with a natal name that was linked together by possessives, like a train by couplings. She was, not merely on account of that but perhaps for a variety of reasons, what many people would have called, and did, a snob. Her provenance wasn't a thing she hid away, as other women might have done, but rather placed in front of you as a reminder of the woman you were dealing with. As she also made apparent, she had an entrée, perhaps originally through her husband, to numerous great men of Oxford, in particular a Warden noted for his wit and classicism, of whom it seemed she was an intimate. Such connections deepened her allure. Both her physical and mental being struck me as intrinsically French in spite of geniture. I had acquired, largely but not entirely through my reading, a sense of what a certain kind of French *dame* might consist of, whereas I knew nothing of the Portuguese. LH was a cultured and intelligent but by no means intellectual or academic model of the kind of small, lean *femme française* who, while not being conventionally what you might find good-looking, has a sympathetic sharpness in which sudden glances of her eyes convey an amicable malice. I was flattered that, independently of her husband, she took an interest in me. She was one of those older women, some of them older than my parents, who at a time when I was unattached and trying to find some sort of passage through the world would seem to take me over and would inform me of my merits and shortcomings with a freedom that was perhaps essentially maternal. Whether I was being considered by her for her daughter was not a question I considered or had any grounds to think I was.

Like GC and NH in their own ways, CH was someone I hoped to be approved by and even to impress, in which my place at Cambridge greatly helped me; it

195

was, I imagine, the reason for his giving up his time to me. Our relationship was that of a pupil with his tutor, although nothing was ever said to this effect. It wasn't in Classics or in Literature that he engaged in my improvement but in Music. Across a courtyard from the old stone house there was a renovated barn that had maintained its feeling of dilapidation. Here he kept the most part of his library, although in the house he also had a study lined with books whose atmosphere was more fixed and set in place as something to be left alone. And as companion pieces he had his creaking rattan armchair and his crackling ancient wireless to which I listened with him when on the Third Programme it might be playing, for example, Haydn. The first time that this happened I naively told him, as evidence of my prowess, how I had taken to Tchaikovsky. He didn't hide his disapproval of my immaturity. The true rewards of music lay in such as Haydn, not in the lush pretences of Romanticism. His severity made me reconsider, although I have found, so many years beyond that lesson, that my taste is neither "classical" nor "romantic" but wherever music reaches deepest.

The library was another vital influence. Those rambling shelves, with books and papers, ancient and modern, of an overall pale brownness, that were squeezed within interstices from floor to ceiling, seemed to convey his soul – though that was orderly, I imagined – and were what I desired one day for myself.

To complete the Latin tag, he took me out with him

on walks up past the butcher's to the hills above the village, which, occupying a wide dip, has long since totally obscured itself within its sprawl of access roads and cul-de-sacs. His route led naturally to Oxford, but well short of it, and I felt the privilege of walking with him and his walking stick, yet at the same time the discomfort of maintaining conversation of an unexceptionable rationality, especially as, like so many highly cerebral people, he was not, I saw, at all unready to maintain a silence, whereas my own anxiety was to fill it.

Some years later, when he was working in Australia and I had come to work in Oxford and was in search of lodgings, LH offered me accommodation on a temporary basis. She didn't want me to begin to feel too comfortable, of which, she soon said, she saw a danger; for my interim accommodation had a great deal to commend it. On the intended length of, or the reasons for, her husband's absence she was unforthcoming, which led me to pose a question to myself I couldn't put to her: had their marriage finally ended in a state of mutual impatience? I knew, from her own acerbic disillusion, that before they had come to Oxfordshire they had lived more grandly outside Winchester, in an immaculate Queen Anne mansion filled with so many bedrooms it must have been three-quarters empty; whereas their present house, whose name was at any rate commensurate with its solidity and which to me was a place of taste and culture, had always fallen short of what she needed, perhaps very naturally in the light of where she came from, for contentment.

Looking back, I see CH as the embodiment of an ageing Oxford academic of the old school, one who had done much with his intelligence and application and yet, in his wife's eyes and perhaps his own, had ultimately failed. He had not achieved enough, or enough of the right sort. He was, though a Fellow of All Souls who had gone into the world and given it his miscellaneous learning, neither the amusing Warden nor the lustrous President of one of the more prestigious Oxford colleges.

JN

So much in a life, forgotten, disappears and is available at best to our surmises, and there are places in a history where only much later can one see or guess at motives lying behind a surface that had been opaque. My relationship with JN, my College's Senior Tutor, may be a case of this. How far and from what point my father was in touch with him, bearing in mind that during all the years I was at Cambridge my father was in Hong Kong, is something I can never know. It wasn't the kind of information that my father shared with me. But JN later told me, when it was safe to do so, that following Part 1, which in my own eyes and JN's had gone off at least acceptably, my father had approached him to have my Part 2 subject altered. He wished me switched to

198

"Social Sciences" or something of that kind. JN did not disturb me with the matter: I continued with my English studies. Nor did my father ever tell me he had taken this initiative that JN had suppressed.

JN was well aware, then, of my separation from my family and of my being one of the youngest in my entry, for which he himself would as much as anyone have been responsible, and so might feel the weight not only of his academic but his moral role. More than that, the nature of my relations with JN and also, since he involved himself directly, the new Master of the College, suggests discreet consideration of my future which, if I had followed up their thinking, would possibly have kept me in the Cambridge world. That later I turned instead to Oxford was, in another context, my unforeseen good fortune, since I met there the woman who has been my wife for over half a century and has been my rock and refuge. And so, although I wasn't long at Oxford, I gained one of its prizes.

On one occasion I had reason to be both grateful to and yet embarrassed by JN. It was during a supervision in his room. There were four or five of us in the group, seated round his table contemplating with bemusement *Spelt from Sibyl's Leaves*. This was not a Hopkins poem I had come across, nor had, it was plain, the others. It was the kind that from its very typographic physiognomy immediately deterred investigation. We had only just begun when we were interrupted by his telephone, to which he was called away, but before he closed the door into his study, which was just beyond, he asked me to "take over". It was a recognition I would very happily have done without, presuming no one else was given it. Evidently the analysis provided in a key book of the 1930s on the new bearings to be found in English poetry was not one any of us had read or, if we had, had any memory of. There was another student there who was likely to have felt aggrieved at my preferment and now put me to the test. Rather than trying to cast light himself on the obscurities, he fired questions at me of a kind it wasn't probable I would relish. Without my having time, though, either to show my mettle or my ignorance, which was the likelier, JN returned and took control again of what remained, concerning Sibyl's Leaves, obscure proceedings.

CL

What is it that decides between particular friendship and a more general amiability? How, from so many young men, numbering well above a hundred, who were entirely strangers, did I become especially attached to two of them when neither was my neighbour but lived in another court and all of us were reading different subjects, though in the Arts? It is easy to say, and true, that I don't remember, but they were drawn also to each other, and I may have met one through the other. The second of them was JB, a sketch of whom comes next.

I was always looking for others who could reinforce

my self-belief. These were naturally people the value of whose endorsement came from my regard for them. CL had the ingredients which met my needs. He was, to begin with, my elder by a year, which at the age we were then had the kind of force that time erodes. While I saw him as more assured than I was he was subject also to despondency, a state of gloom that while it made him more withdrawn rendered him also more accessible. He got on generally well and easily with other people, which brought him standing. And for me he showed an affection and regard which, though he has long since slipped away, remain with me as my essential memory of our friendship.

It was early in our second year that his consideration saw me through discomfort. My accommodation was a long way from the city centre in an anonymous small brick house somewhere on a large dispiriting estate, my room placed on the ground floor just below the one in which presumably the landlady, an unresponsive single mother in her early thirties, had her bedroom, from which at night my ceiling shook and thumped with her invisible amours. Early each morning, as soon as I had finished breakfast, which she brought to me in my room, I retreated on my bicycle to become, with his indulgence, CL's daytime lodger in his own superior accommodation, which was the property of the College. My imposition of myself contrived my rescue; for the next term his landlady, who at once had treated me as one of "hers", gave over to me in the fullness of her generous heart a little room, a neighbour to the eaves, which she had always kept, I understood, for her potential visitors, of whom I never saw or heard her mention any. Into this I moved with the degree of joy that only those who yesterday were in the same degree of misery can reach.

There was, however, a circumstance in which our judgements differed, and which had a negative bearing on his largely sunny disposition. This was in the case of women. For he chose women who controlled him and with no light touch and who when we were all together turned him to a faded copy of the self we knew. Then he was neither cheery nor amusing. Soon after Cambridge days, when I had gone to teach in Africa, I had a letter from him telling me that, having fully realised the disaffection he had come to feel, he had broken off what I had feared was an unbreakable engagement to a woman who had always chilled me. My too enthusiastic answer showed impetuous naivety. His reaction, which I heard about not from him (it was a subject that we never mentioned) but from another friend, JB, to whom he had revealed the hurt that I had caused him, was as if, while he could let himself reject her, he could not allow me to have endorsed his judgement prior to his having made it.

There had been, however, a previous occasion, at the end of our years in Cambridge, when – over a woman – he hadn't hurt so much as galled me. He had poured cold water on my unanticipated triumph, the sudden acquisition of an idol of those days, a Swedish blonde with all the driving purpose of her looks, her culture and her knowledge – a girl who while younger than me by some way was, I suspect, my elder in experience. I had, however, already a spirit of adventure that, fighting against my natural caution, was hidden generally from view. She didn't remove this tension but weighed the scales down on her own side. Having met her only later, CL informed me with a smile combining hubris with regret that if he had been in Cambridge at the time I should have lacked the cause I seemed to have for so much satisfaction.

I think of him still, though gone so long because divorced from me by geography and women, with gratitude and fondness.

JB

JB was, I see now, reflecting on it dispassionately rather than with the disappointment that our friendship brought me and him too finally, one of my life's key benefactors. Its having begun at all still seems to me perhaps implausible. JB, as we arrived at Cambridge, was from my perspective surely too well set both in other peoples' minds and in his own for me to see him as a likely friend, and he similarly was unlikely to be drawn to my obscurity. The very gap there was between us in our natures and our records pointed surely to our incompatibility. Yet though gaps may be dividing they may also, in some cases, rouse a certain interest, and I was ready to be malleable to accommodate myself to how he saw the world, an initiative that may have passed him by not only in its subtlety but in my keenness to identify with him. As I grew, however, to know him better I came to see the satisfaction that he found in bringing in stray sheep and, like a genial shepherd, leading them to more nutritious pastures – not that by then I would have put myself within this needy category or would have assumed that he did.

He was made for and accustomed to command. It was said of him, with friendly irony by a close relation, that as the head boy of his public school he had been more important even than its Master. He didn't much care for having to contend with rivals. He needed an existence of control both of events and people, in which ideally he could employ his geniality and generosity. Thus when after I had quit my aunt and no longer had a home in the vacations he shared his with me, in addition to his mother and his father and his younger siblings. Some years after this, when he was married and I once more adrift, he was again my saviour, and I joined him and his understanding and accommodating wife in London. Here the three of us lived a year together in the cordial manner of a Haydn trio, with JB as its leading instrument.

In the years that followed, when I too was married, we were separated geographically and became so also in spirit. This distance of our spirits was something that

I grew aware of through an accretion of discomforts and humiliations that his grievances imposed upon me. I had become too free of him in a manner that he wasn't used to and seemed to him like a betrayal, notably in its occupation of a territory he had once commanded. I had been, in his perception as I see it, unfaithful to my old self, whose unthreatening capacities and potentialities he had been able to accommodate. There were one or two improvements in my circumstances that, his reactions to them made apparent, he saw as stealing an illicit march on him, the normality having always been to his advantage and our friendship being based upon an inequality that was tacit. It was as if I had acquired, by means that might be questionable, a position and a situation that went beyond what he conceded to me. But my old self had been merely moving on to ground that had more room and scope in it. To him, however, my reach had entered a terrain he had thought of as his own and from which it wasn't that he had been dislodged but that he had dislodged himself.

Against my own experience of him I also noted, through the years, some friendships that he had in which he took a role that was subordinate and deferential. These were invariably with men who were a little older and whose positions and assurance he respected.

In him from the beginning liberalism and conservatism had debated with each other. His being was grounded in a conservatism that his liberalism, strengthened by the growing impact of his profession on his nature, was eroding. In his own perception he remained, no doubt, a liberal conservative, but the balance had altered with events and influences and, as it appeared to me, the noun and adjective had changed their places.

His importance to me was considerable and our inevitable unravelling something much regretted.

JL

JL belongs to my first year in Africa, when I was twenty-one. He was in the Peace Corps and some years my elder. His father, I believe, was linked with the World Bank.

I met him on my arrival in the middle of that great region of Nigeria's north which makes its way to the Sahara. He was sharing a bungalow with a fellow member of the Peace Corps, with whom his patience had come near to running out. He was, JL informed me, gauche and inconsiderate and, as I came to realise as I got to know JL, would not have understood what drove him. Their bungalow was a short way from my own, which made for some initial separation. He seized, however, on an opportunity to move into a bungalow next door and through a hedge, and after this I saw much more of him.

He was a person I very soon relied on for a sense of comfort and protection. He hadn't merely a spirit of adventure but actively engaged in it: he had driven far beyond Nigeria's edges to the deserts of the Upper Volta and Niger. And in the manner of a chaperone he took me with him into places that, at the beginning, I would never have dared enter on my own. He had come to Africa not only motivated to give help but, more inwardly, to search into his nature and identity. He made every effort possible. He wore, at weekends, the babariga or long robe, and in the bars and night clubs danced to the Ghanaian and Nigerian music which was itself a combination of America and Africa. I am not sure that at the time I fully grasped the depth of purpose lying behind this change of clothing. To me, both young and ignorant of the USA, it wore an air of pantomime: he was, wasn't he, an American in fancy dress? Of course, I never made the slightest comment on it, and neither did he to me, but the truth was that he was laying claim to some Nigerian identity while shedding some of his American. His dress was an expression of a longing for osmosis.

He went deep and wide in searching for himself, but despite his ardour there was nothing to be found. Perhaps he had been looking in the wrong places? Perhaps he should have sought a posting further south towards the delta? Knowing his failure, and in a state of disillusionment, he applied to go home early, a procedure not in keeping with the Peace Corps' rules and spirit, and it was in a querulous, frustrated manner that he left Nigeria.

JL was a man of moods and glooms on whom I much

depended for my own feeling of security, such as it amounted to. He was emotional and passionate and at risk always of being disappointed. It was only after he had gone I saw it was in me, a young, uncertain Englishman largely unacquainted with his culture, he had achieved some sort of audience and perhaps an echo of his own voice that he had been unable to discover in the imagined *patria* he had been so fruitlessly exploring. And I had found in him a person I could more easily confide in than the run of my compatriots. I should like to think that, in considering his failure, as he deemed it, to identify with Africa or to be admitted by it, he was able to take some compensatory satisfaction in the friendship he had shared with me, an Englishman, whose eyes were just then opening wider to the changing world.

CO

It was Cambridge that arranged that we should meet. Soon after I had reached Nigeria, CO approached me in the common room. That first encounter at a staff room table in which, with consummate grace, he offered me his friendship as a fellow Cambridge man, I recall as if we were still standing there, though it was nearly sixty years ago. If NH was crucially the one who showed me into literature, who more vitally than CO, with the benefit of a decade's more experience than mine and a more worldly nature to enjoy it, could be said to have shown me into life? Who was it who shocked his confreres by subjecting the ideal of "négritude", which was the creation of Senghor, to the dismissive laughter of a universalist whose culture was a synthesis of Igbo, English, Greek and Latin? He stood against contemporary orthodoxy on behalf of the fluidity of literature, as is demonstrated in his work. Small and lithe, he used laughter as others might employ a foil. Once, to my discomfort, when I dared to show him some of my attempts at writing, he "laughed his head off" at a line that I had written which I found out later much resembled, in its imagery and rhythm, one of his. Perhaps the difference was a matter of sophistication, so that while his, that of a thirty-one-year-old, had emotionally some clothes on, mine, that of someone ten years younger, was more vulnerably naked.

On New Year's morning, 1963 he drove me at electrifying speed, his fingers as airy on the wheel as swallows on the water of a pool, all the way to Lagos from Ibadan, a matter of ninety or a hundred miles, to greet his dear chum Chinua Achebe, who was busy writing at his dining table when we interrupted him, and perhaps had not expected either CO or his satellite, for we spent our visit standing a bit behind him and on either side like servers in attendance on a vicar.

CO might sometimes disappear inside himself but had also such vivacity that, if you didn't know him, you might discount the possibility that he was as much an introvert as the "live wire" who was so good at

209

entertaining you, and perhaps was more the former than the latter. How else would he have been an artist – a poet of the kind he was, deliberating on the insides of those rhythms to which Eliot had contributed? For there were places in his earliest published work, of which, when I was staying with him for the first time in Ibadan, he gave me, "with the author's compliments", a copy, that have echoes as well as thefts – wasn't it Eliot himself who validated thefts? – exhibiting his provenance. To me, who worshipped in the church of T.S. Eliot, the influence was a holy one.

Yet the live wire in him was charged with an energy that was iconoclastic. He lived in general as if whatever rules and regulations had been manufactured by officialdom were of not the least validity or even casual interest for him. His code of ethics, of whose kindness I was a grateful beneficiary, was his own particular recipe. Culturally and morally I found myself emancipated by him up to the limit that my cautious nature could permit me. Of all my mentors he has been perhaps the one most radical in his effect on how I see the world.

Later, but not so long beyond my own departure, his political disaffection, which he had always had, caused him to be implicated as a civilian in the abortive military coup of January, 1966 in which the Northern Nigerian Premier, Sir Ahmadu Bello, the man who pulled the strings in Lagos, was assassinated. There was a sombre personal irony for me in this. Only a few years earlier I had been invited by CO to join him at the publication by the Cambridge Press of this same leader's memoir of his life in politics. And so at Lugard Hall, the government buildings in Kaduna, we had queued together to receive our copies from Sir Ahmadu's own hands.

Later he had joined up as a major in the civil war of 1967. I next encountered him entirely by chance, in the misplaced comfort of an Aldwych library, where I read in that day's paper of his brutal ending, gunned down and obliterated, in the forests of his origins. His death was where his life had taken him, and he became a martyr and an icon for those who like him had stood naked before Idoto.

My close association with him, and perhaps also with JL, and also perhaps my link with a particular woman, appears to have reignited MI6's previous interest in my future, for it seems they had been keeping watch on me and thought, as they told me in a letter, that I had had an "interesting time in Africa". The woman, who was multiply remarkable, encountered CO also, through the theatre, in which both of them were active. But that is another subject, in another history.

RO

RO, also my senior by ten years, was the mentor of my thirties and my guide in art and painting. In debate he was dogmatic and intransigent. It took courage, which I sometimes had, to question his antipathies, so that when he castigated Auerbach or Pasmore one was hesitant to question him even if one's honest reason was only to discover what he thought was wrong with Auerbach or Pasmore.

RO had been Bomberg's pupil. Bomberg's influence on his painting was beyond my means to judge, but failed to come over to me on the surface. His work was abstract and done with a strength that sometimes pleased me and sometimes didn't. My wife once gave me for my birthday a charcoal he had done, a semi-figurative portrait of a girl sitting on a chair which was then and remains a beautiful aesthetic object.

He earned his living not from his paintings, which neither sold sufficiently nor offered him the necessary reputation, but as a teacher who suffered on a constant basis at the hands of the obtuse, and they no less at his hands. At least I had, as others seemingly hadn't, the excuse of claiming ignorance in painting, which was a half if not three-quarters truth but enabled him to make allowances indicative of generosity. Besides, unlike his students I had no formal obligation to show progress, although I was always at great risk of being tested. His masters were Cezanne, Matisse and Ingres. As to others I was never sure. Through him I entered more definitively that part of the world of painting that he could acknowledge. The failure of his painting to achieve the recognition that he thought it should have caused him to be subject to the darkest moods from which it wasn't generally possible to lift him.

There was a quid pro quo in our exchanges. His interest in some literature and some writers made for a measure of equality, at least in subject matter, for a conversation could be satisfactorily ended only if he found he could accept my argument. There was a link with CO through the regard that RO had for Eliot. But I was forced to hold firm against him and his wife in a dispute, less horticultural than poetic, over the poet's use of lilacs and their insistence that instead of "now that lilacs are in bloom" it would have been much better if he'd written "now that April is in bloom", and when the word turned up at least twice more, for perfectly good reasons, and moreover was detected lurking at the very outset of the work he is most known by possibly, RO's wife, to sum up, said:

'I had never realised that, in him, lilacs were so ubiquitous.'

And they smiled in concert at her jeu d'esprit.

At last our friendship, always on an edge, irreparably fractured. Rather than of that I think of his importance to me and the kindness that, when hard times came, I had from both of them. His ending carried an ironic pathos. After he had died unrecognised, his wife, who had long since given up her own art for the duties of a housewife and a mother, quickly achieved on her return to it a notice and celebrity her husband's epic zeal had been denied.

DF

I see it as my good luck that, from the days when I was learning Latin and had not yet parted company with Science, one friend has come the distance with me. To this numerous factors have no doubt contributed, but the key one, I am claiming, is the sense we each have had of our equality. The balance, if perhaps at moments it has wavered, whether in one direction or another, but hardly at all and hardly ever, has stayed essentially as horizontal as the lines across this page. Yet, like so many things that happen to endure, our friendship had a provenance which made it an historical improbability: for while in the war I had a father serving in the British Army DF's was serving in the German, and while I began life in the dark surroundings of industrial Yorkshire DF began it in the rural light of eastern Germany, and while my home was a minute one in a terrace DF's was an enormous mansion with a vast estate. DF is, however, through his mother as intrinsically an Englishman as it is surely possible to be, and even in this latest century belongs in spirit to the eighteenth, conducting everything he has to do with as if it were still in situ and he within it. And when we are all four together – he and I and M and V our wives – it's as if we ourselves were actually the instruments that resonated with the cheerful string quartets of Haydn.